# Welland Ontario Book 2 in Colour Photos, Saving Our History One Photo at a Time

Photography
by Barbara Raué
2016

Series Name:
Cruising Ontario

Book 139: Welland Book 2

Cover photo: 201 Niagara Street – Cooper Mansion, Page 32

# Series Name: Cruising Ontario
## Saving Our History One Photo at a Time
## in colour photos

Books Available in Alphabetical Order:
Aberfoyle, Acton, Alton, Ancaster, Arthur, Aylmer, Ayr, Bloomingdale, Brantford, Burlington, Caledon, Caledonia, Cambridge, Clifford, Conestogo, Delhi, Dorchester to Aylmer, Drayton, Drumbo, Dundas, Eden Mills, Elmira, Elora, Fergus, Guelph, Hagersville, Hamilton, Hanover, Harriston, Hespeler, Jarvis, Kitchener, Linwood, Listowel, London, Lucknow, Mono, Mount Forest, Neustadt, New Hamburg, Niagara-on-the-Lake, Oakville, Orangeville, Orillia, Owen Sound, Palmerston, Peterborough, Port Elgin, Preston, Rockwood, Seaforth, Sheffield, Shelburne, Simcoe, Southampton, St. Jacobs, St. Thomas, Stoney Creek, Stratford, Tillsonburg, Waterdown, Waterford, Waterloo, Wellesley, Wingham

Book 114-116: Waterloo
Book 117-119: Windsor
Book 120: Amherstburg
Book 122: Essex
Book 123-124: Kingsville
Book 125-127: Woodstock
Book 128: Thamesford
Book 129: St. Mary's
Book 133-136: Sarnia
Book 137: Petrolia
Book 138-139: Welland

# Other Books by Barbara Raue

Coins of Gold

Arrows, Indians and Love

The Life and Times of Barbara
Volume 1: Inventions That Have Enhanced My Life
Volume 2: Entertainment That I Have Enjoyed
Volume 3: East Coast Trips
Volume 4: Olympics Have Always Intrigued Me
Volume 5: Wonders of the World
Volume 6: Caribbean Cruises We Have Enjoyed
Volume 7: Animals
Volume 8: Storms and Other Major Disasters in My Lifetime
Volume 9: Wars, Terrorist Attacks and Major Disasters

The Cromwell Family Book

Laura Secord Discovered

Daddy Where Are You?

Visit Barbara's website to view all of her books
http://barbararaue.ca

# Table of Contents

Welland, named after the Welland River in England, is located in the center of Niagara. Within a half-hour, residents can travel to Niagara Falls, Niagara-on-the-Lake, St. Catharines, Port Colborne or Buffalo. It has been traditionally known as the place *where rails and water meet*, referring to the railways from Buffalo to Toronto and Southwestern Ontario, and the waterways of the Welland Canal and Welland River, which played a great role in the city's development. The city was first settled in 1788 by United Empire Loyalists.

Welland, because of its proximity to the Sir Adam Beck hydroelectric station at Niagara Falls, was historically known for its steel, automotive, and textile industries. Manufacturing firms were the biggest employers in Welland, with companies like Union Carbide, United Steel, Plymouth Cordage Company, three drop forges, a cotton mill, and the Atlas Steel Company, as well as general manufacturing plants, influencing the shaping of early Welland.

The Plymouth Cordage Company was the first major industrial company to open a plant in Welland in 1906. It was a rope making company with headquarters in Plymouth, Massachusetts; it became the largest manufacturer of rope and twine in the world. Plymouth binder twine was popular among farmers to package farm crops such as grass, wheat and straw, and was the inspiration for the naming of the Plymouth brand of automobiles first produced in 1928. Many workers who relocated to Welland from the company's operations in Plymouth were of Italian origin. To minimise the potential effects of cultural and language barriers, Plymouth Cordage sent four foremen to Welland: one was Italian, one was French, one was German and one was English.

The city is separated by the Welland River and Welland Canal which links Lake Erie and Lake Ontario. The Welland Canal is a ship canal and has been involved in the history of the area ever since the First Welland Canal was extended to reach Lake Erie in 1833. Traversing the Niagara Peninsula from Port Weller to Port Colborne, the canal forms a key section of the St. Lawrence Seaway, enabling ships to ascend and descend the Niagara Escarpment and bypass Niagara Falls. About 40,000,000 tonnes of cargo are carried through the Welland Canal annually by traffic of about 3,000 ocean and Great Lakes vessels. The original canal and its successors allowed goods from Great Lakes ports such as Cleveland, Detroit, and Chicago, as well as heavily industrialized areas of the United States and Ontario, to be shipped to the port of Montreal or to Quebec City, where they were reloaded onto ocean-going vessels for international shipping.

Prior to the Welland By-Pass project, the Welland Canal cut through the centre of Welland. As a result, a very prominent split was created between the east side and the west side of the city. The west side grew primarily to the north and became the most affluent, while the east side expanded south. The Welland By-Pass project, started in 1967 and finished in 1973, provided a new, shorter alignment for the Welland Canal by removing it from downtown Welland to the outskirts of the city. With the completion of the bypass, the east end of Welland became a man-made island, lying between the new and old canal channels. The old alignment of the canal was renamed the Welland Recreational Waterway with the purpose of developing several recreational facilities and tourist attractions along its shores.

In 1914, a local business called Empire Cotton Mills was bought by a Quebec-based company. They brought in twenty francophone families to work in the mill, giving a start to a French-speaking community still very alive in the city today. The Atlas Steel Co. was founded in the 1920s. Roy H. Davis and partners bought the Welland plant from its American shareholders in 1928. Gun barrels were produced here during the Second World War.

## Welland Canal

The first canal ran from Port Dalhousie on Lake Ontario south along Twelve Mile Creek to St. Catharines. From there it took a winding route up the Niagara Escarpment through Merritton to Thorold, where it continued south via Allanburg to Port Robinson on the Welland River. Ships went east (downstream) on the Welland River to Chippewa, at the south (upper) end of the old portage road, where they made a sharp right turn into the Niagara River, upstream towards Lake Erie.

A southern extension from Port Robinson opened in 1833, with the founding of Port Colborne. This extension followed the Welland River south to Welland, and then split to run south to Port Colborne on Lake Erie. A feeder canal ran southwest from Welland to another point on Lake Erie, just west of Rock Point Provincial Park. With the opening of the extension, the canal stretched forty-four kilometres (twenty-seven miles) between the two lakes, with forty wooden locks. Deterioration of the wood used in the locks and the increasing size of ships led to demand for the Second Welland Canal, which used cut stone locks.

### Second Welland Canal

Work began to deepen the canal and to reduce the number of locks to twenty-seven, each 45.7 by 8.1 meters (150 by 27 feet). By 1848, a 2.7 meter (8.9 feet) deep path was completed through the Welland Canal and the rest of the way to the Atlantic Ocean via the St. Lawrence Seaway.

### Third Welland Canal

In 1887, a new shorter alignment was completed between St. Catharines and Port Dalhousie. One of the most interesting features of this third Welland Canal was the Merritton Tunnel on the Grand Trunk Railway line that ran under the canal at Lock 18. Another tunnel carried the canal over a sunken section of the St. David's Road. The new route had a minimum depth of 4.3 meters (14 feet) with twenty-six stone locks, each 82.3 meters (270 feet) long by 13.7 meters (45 feet) wide. Even so, the canal was still too small for many boats.

### Fourth Welland Canal

Construction on the current canal began in 1913 and was officially opened on August 6, 1932. Dredging to the planned twenty-five foot depth was not completed until 1935. The route was again changed north of St. Catharines, now running directly north to Port Weller. There are eight locks, seven at the Niagara Escarpment and the eighth at Port Colborne to adjust with the varying water depth in Lake Erie. The depth was now 7.6 meters (25 feet), with locks 233.5 meters (766 feet) long by 24.4 meters (80 feet) wide.

### Welland By-Pass

In the 1950s, with the building of the present St. Lawrence Seaway, a standard depth of 8.2 meters (27 feet) was adopted. The 13.4-kilometre (8.3 mile) long Welland By-Pass, built between 1967 and 1972, opened for the 1973 shipping season, providing a new and shorter alignment between Port Robinson and Port Colborne and by-passing downtown Welland. All three crossings of the new alignment were built as tunnels.

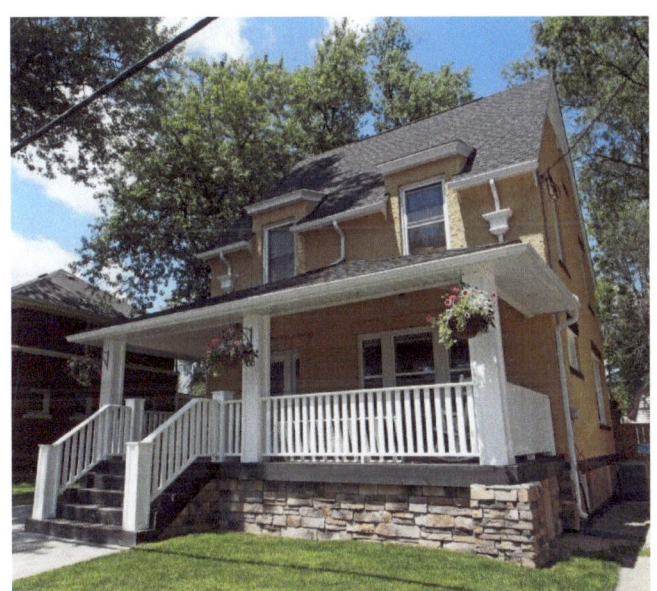

66 Hooker Street

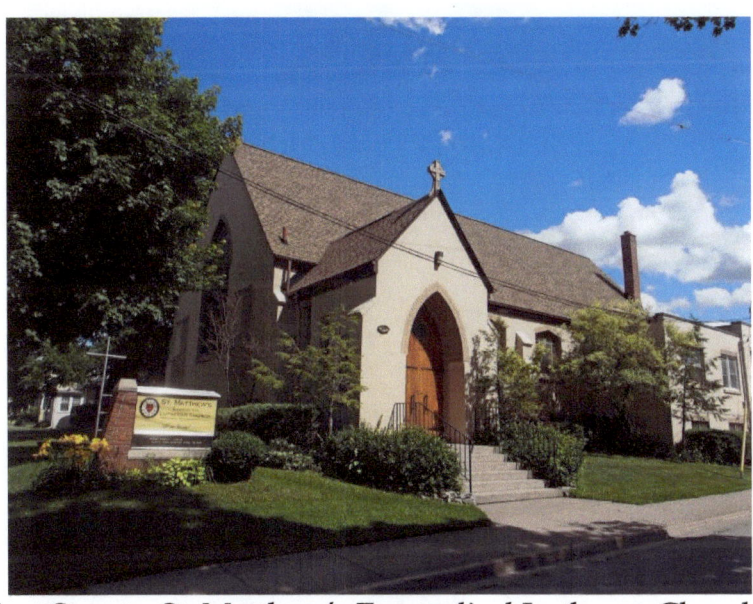

Kent Street – St. Matthew's Evangelical Lutheran Church –
1876 - Gothic

King Street – Merritt Park (named after the founder of the Welland Canal, William Hamilton Merritt) - Welland Canal Memorial Monument is a tribute to all immigrants and those who came from many parts of Canada to make the Welland Ship Canal a reality; their labours and sacrifices laid the foundation for Welland

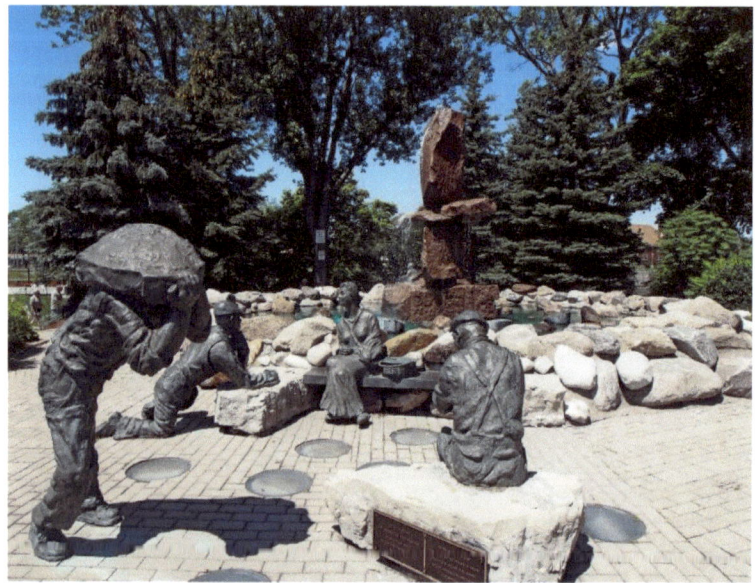

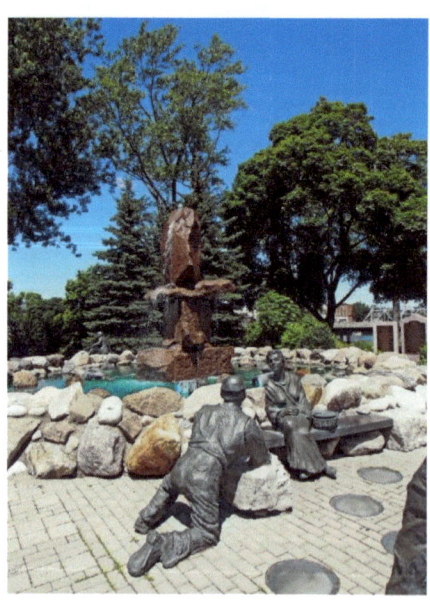

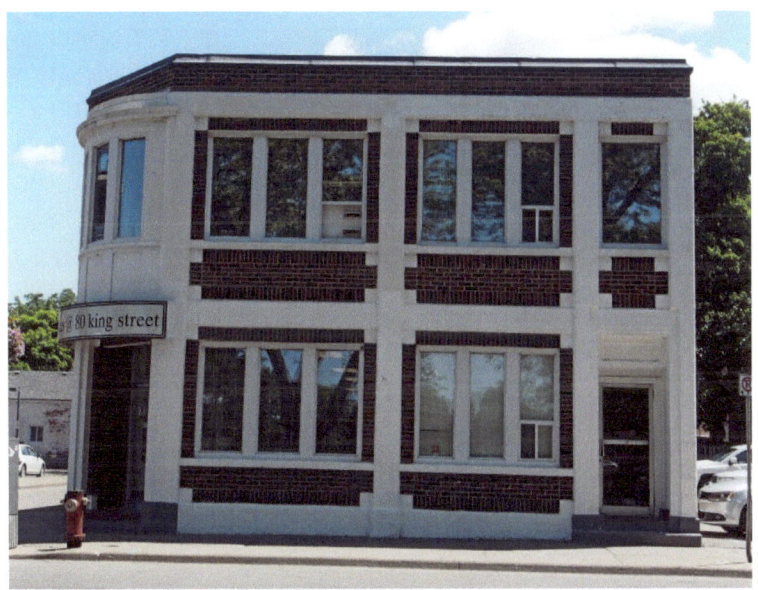

80 King Street

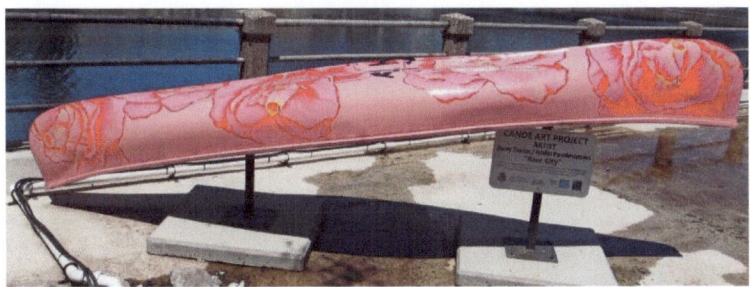

Canoe Art Project – artist Stacey Thomas - "Rose City"

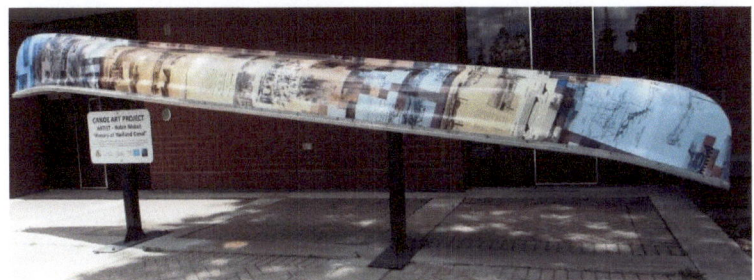

Artist Robin Nisbet – "History of Welland Canal"

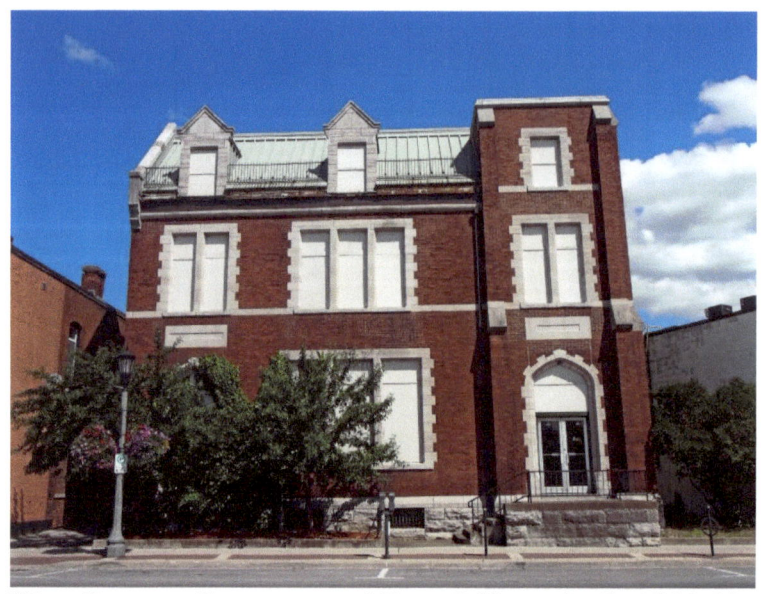

King Street – Customs and Post Office – built 1901-02 – quoining, buttresses, dormers

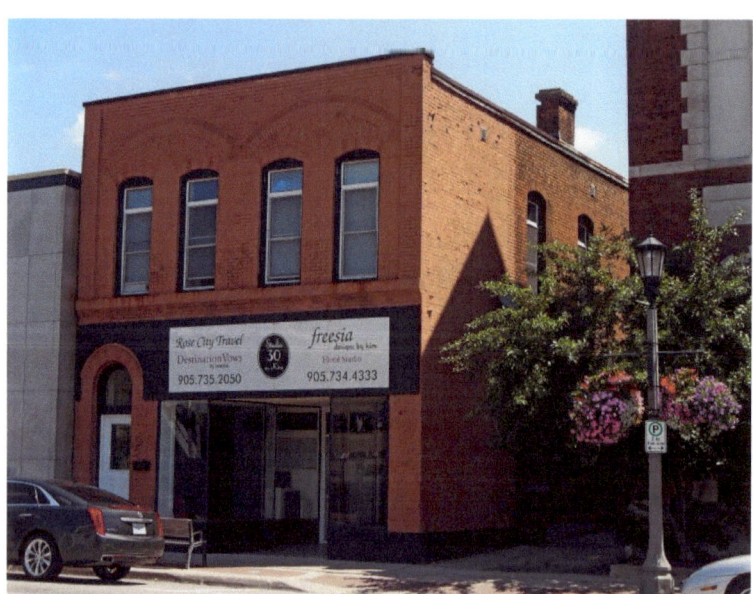

30 King Street – decorative brick arrangement above second floor windows

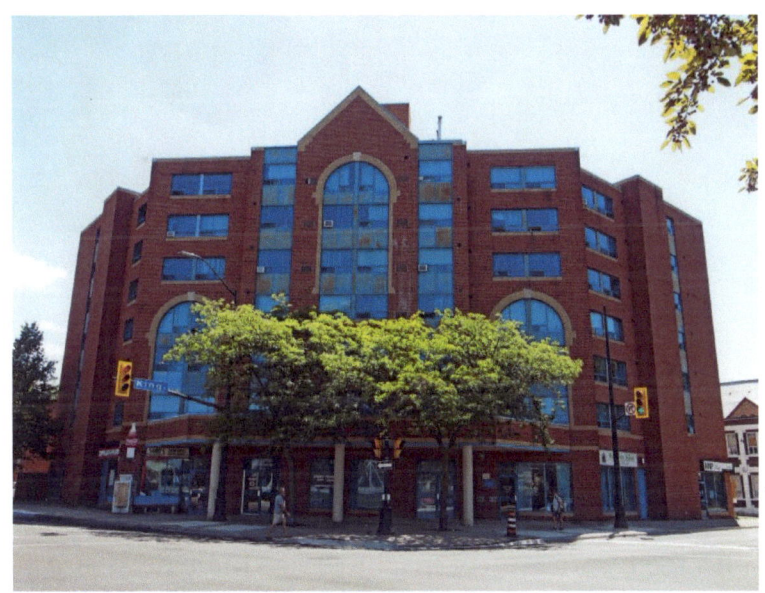

60 King Street

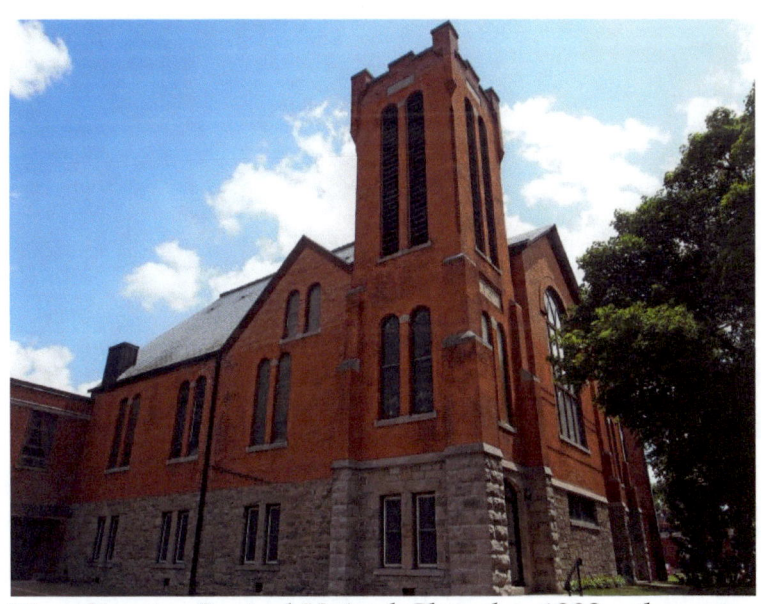

88 King Street – Central United Church – 1908 – three-storey
Romanesque Revival style - four-sided brick bell tower
survives from the original construction in 1882

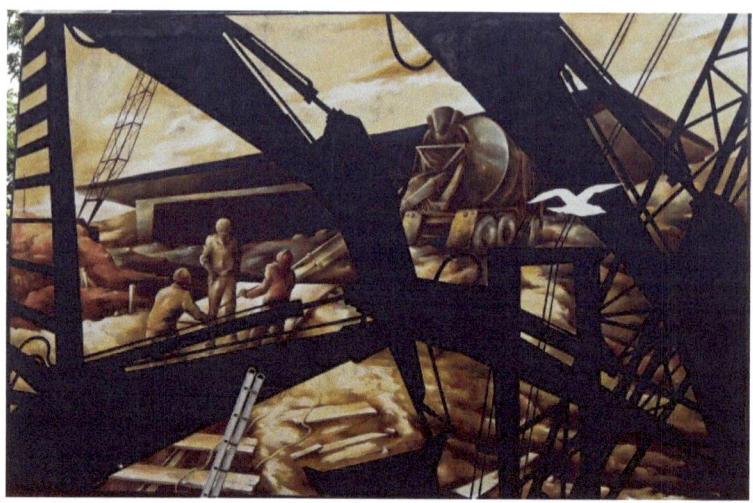

140 King Street – Welland Canal Construction mural – portrays the impression of machinery as huge dark insects in comparison to the small size of man

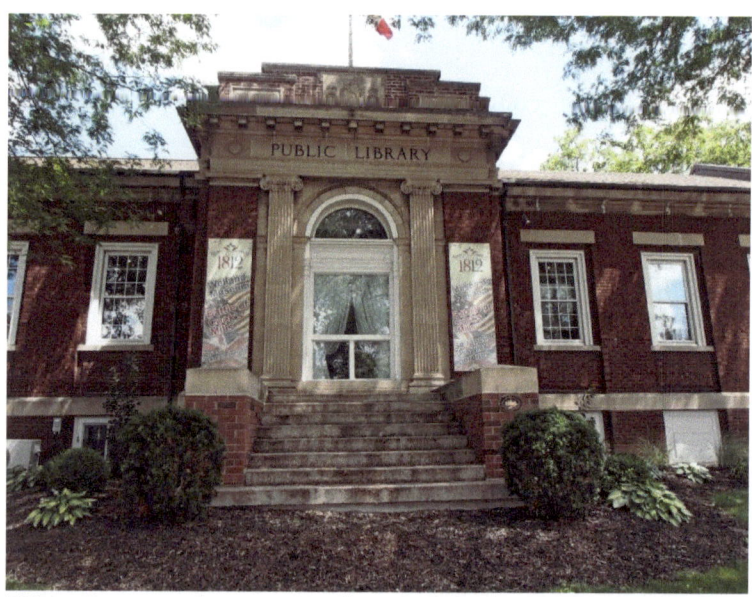

140 King Street – former Welland Public Library – 1923 – dark red Milton brick and Indiana limestone in the Beaux-Arts style

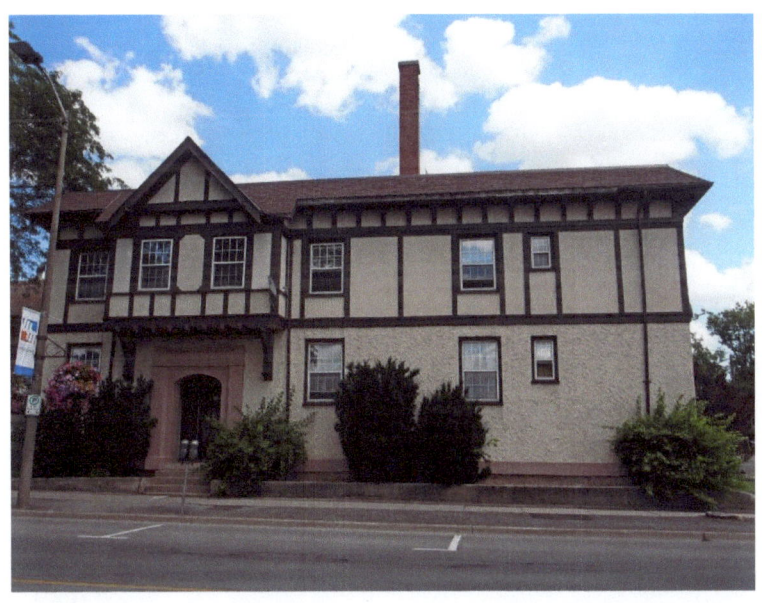

144 King Street – Tudor style

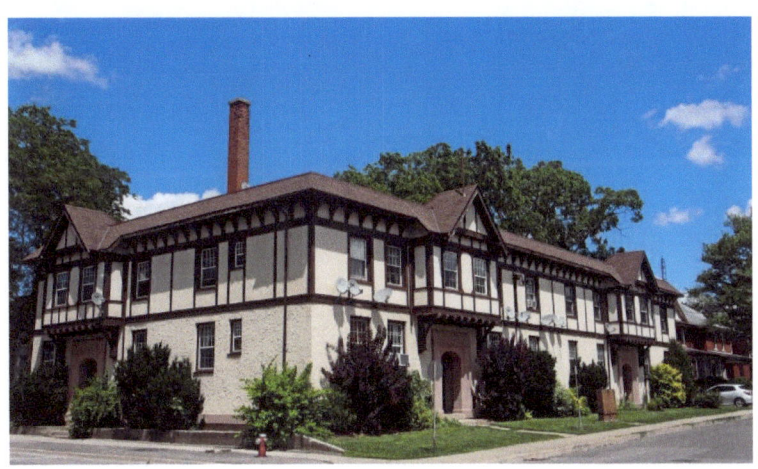

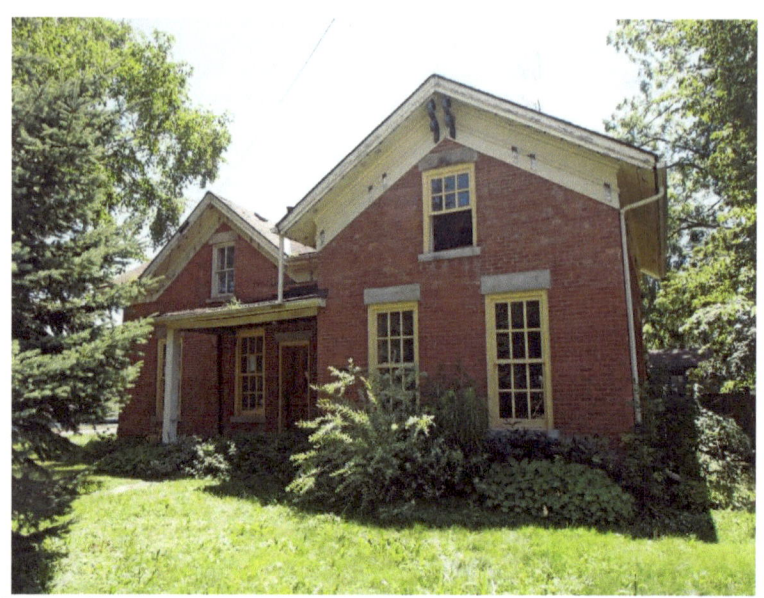

33 Maple Avenue – The Hooker House - 1856 – two-storey
Ontario vernacular, built for Thaddeus W. Hooker

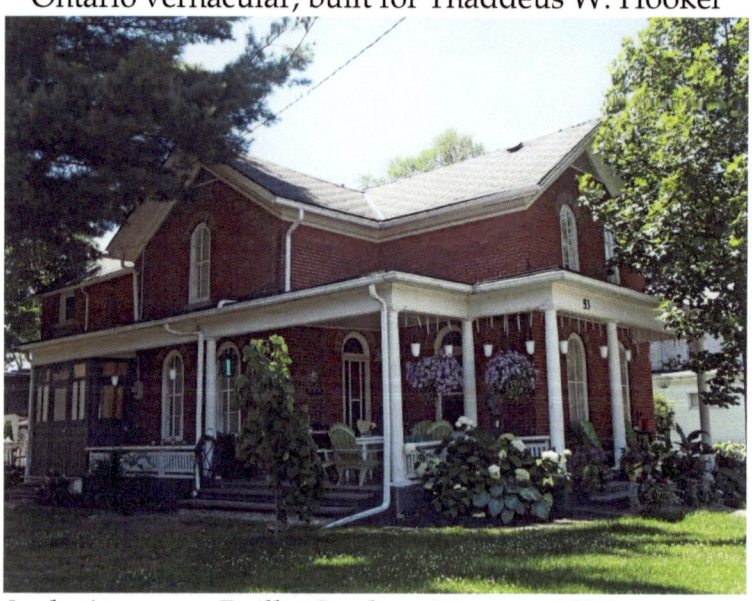

53 Maple Avenue – Reilly-Coulson House – 1873 – two-storey,
red brick, wide eaves, and narrow round-arched windows
capped with buff brick – characteristics of the Italianate style

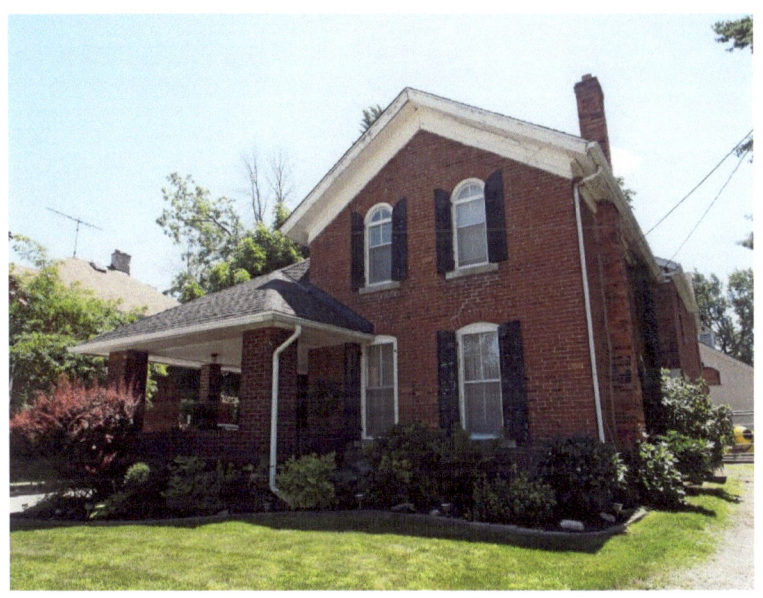

47 Maple Avenue – Sidey-LaRose House – two-storey house with Italianate elements such as the semi-circular and elliptically-arched windows and decorative frieze

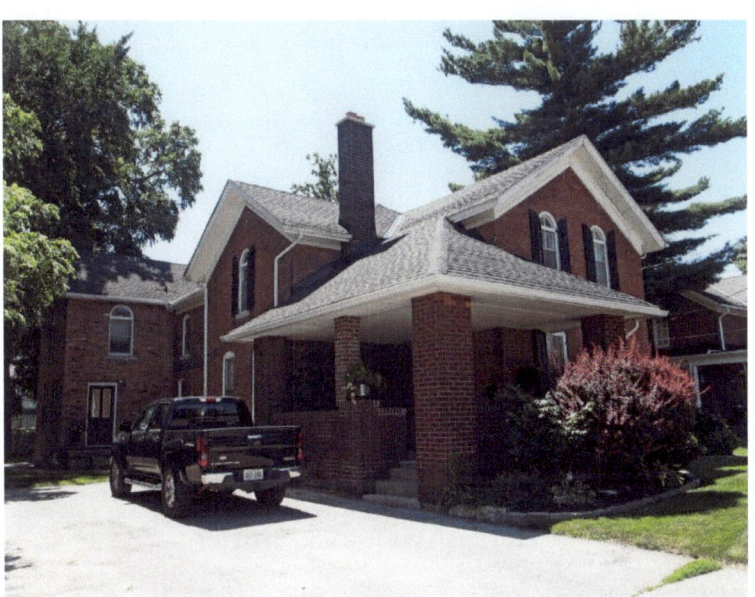

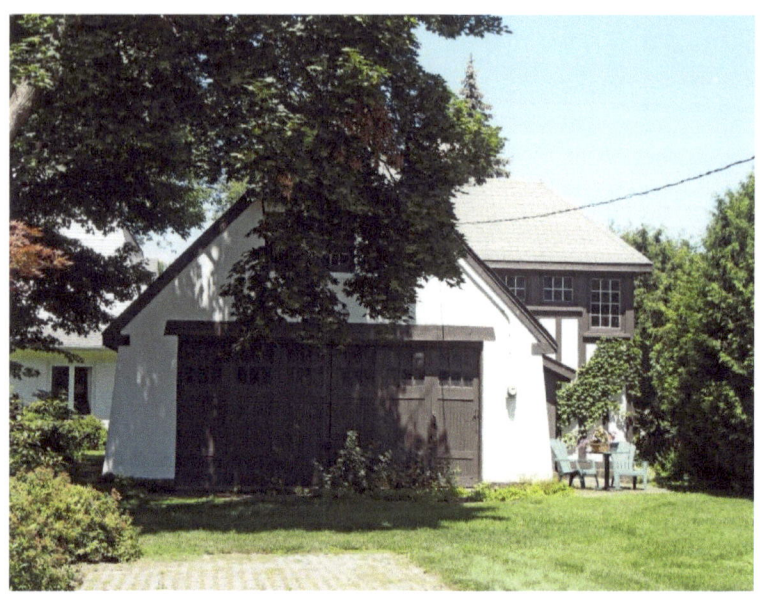

West of 54 Maple Avenue – Coach House for 41 Frazer Street – 1920 – Tudor style

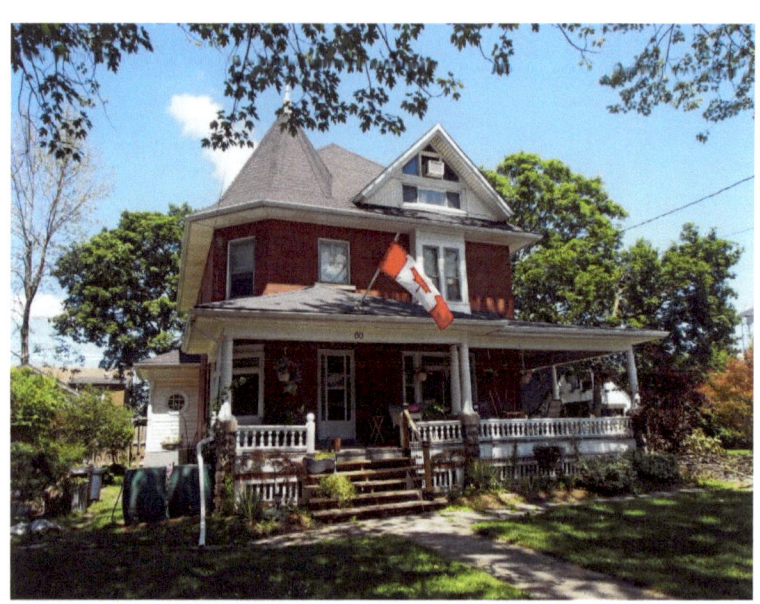

60 Maple Avenue - Victorian

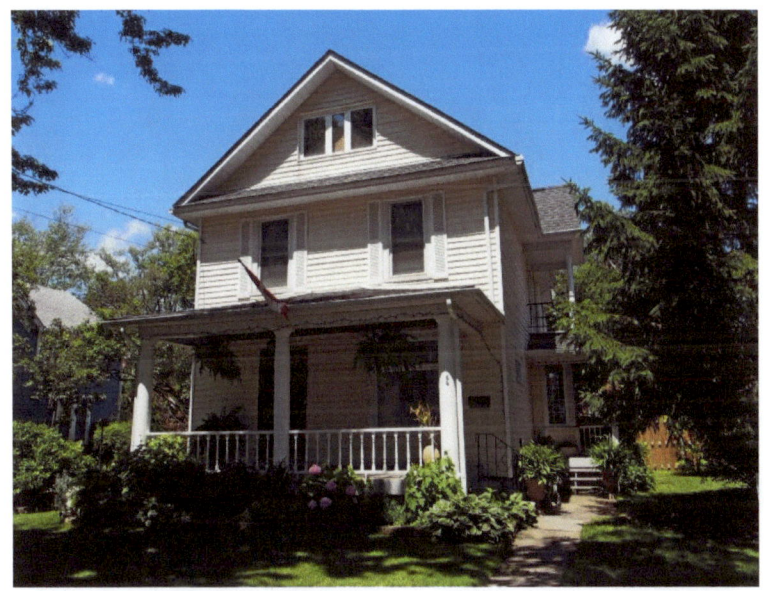

66 Maple Avenue - Edwardian

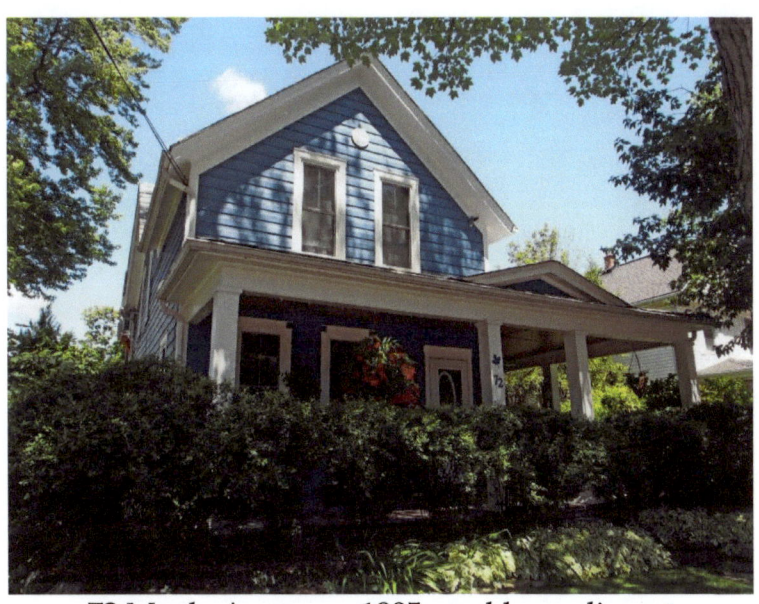

72 Maple Avenue – 1905 – gable, pediment

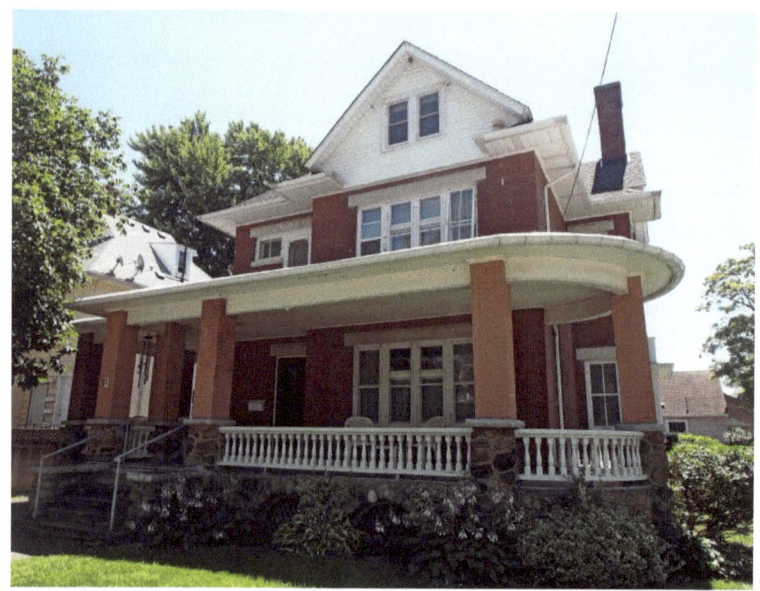

73 Maple Avenue – Italianate, wraparound square-pillared verandah

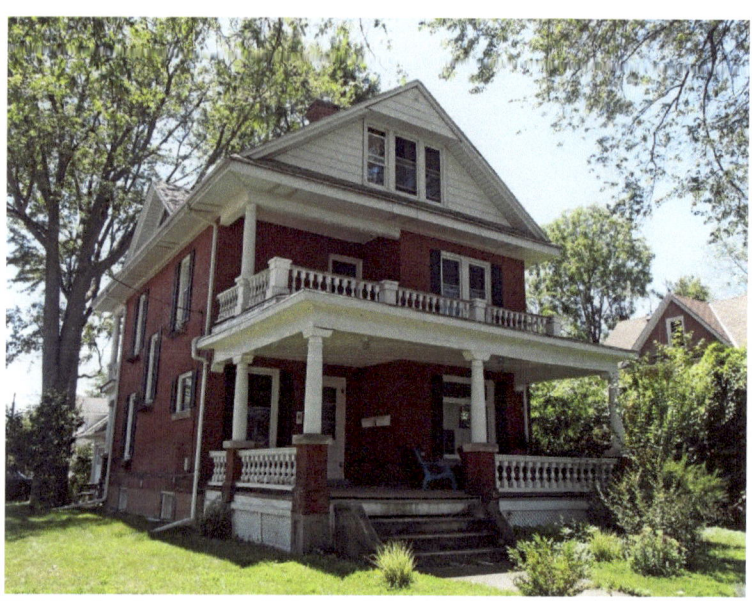

83 Maple Avenue – Edwardian – second floor verandah

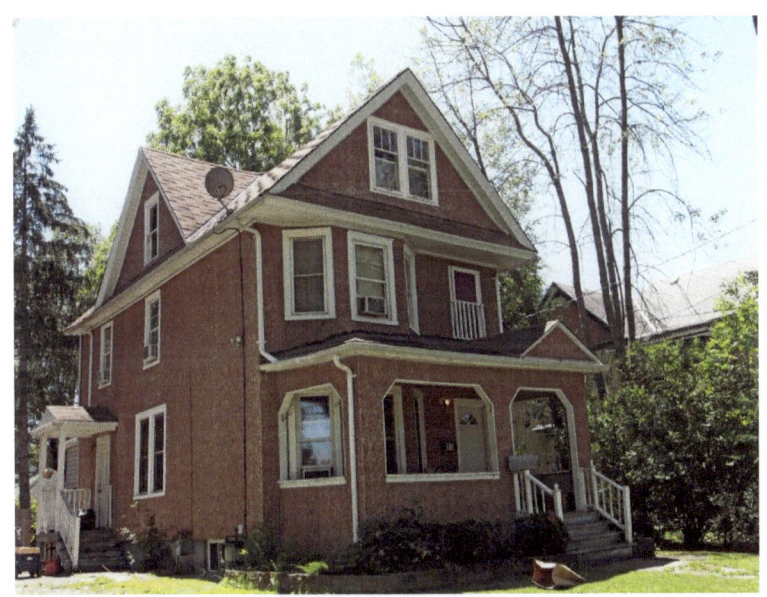

93 Maple Avenue

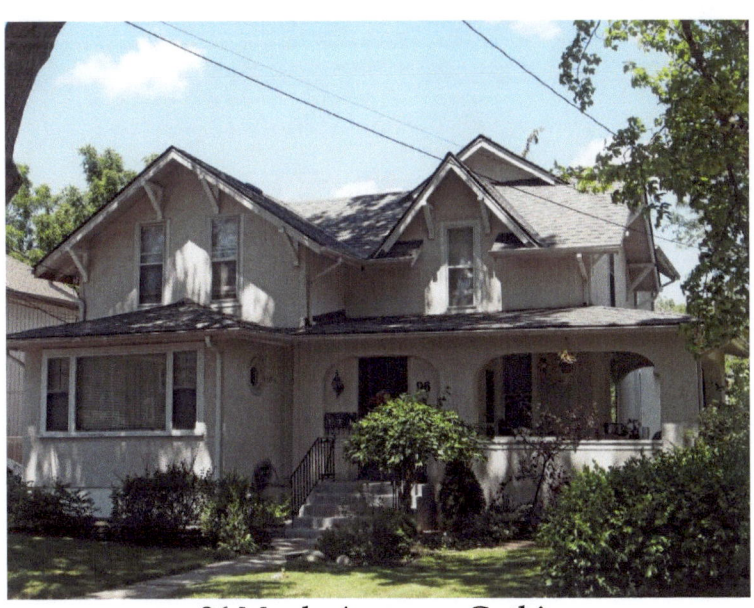

96 Maple Avenue - Gothic

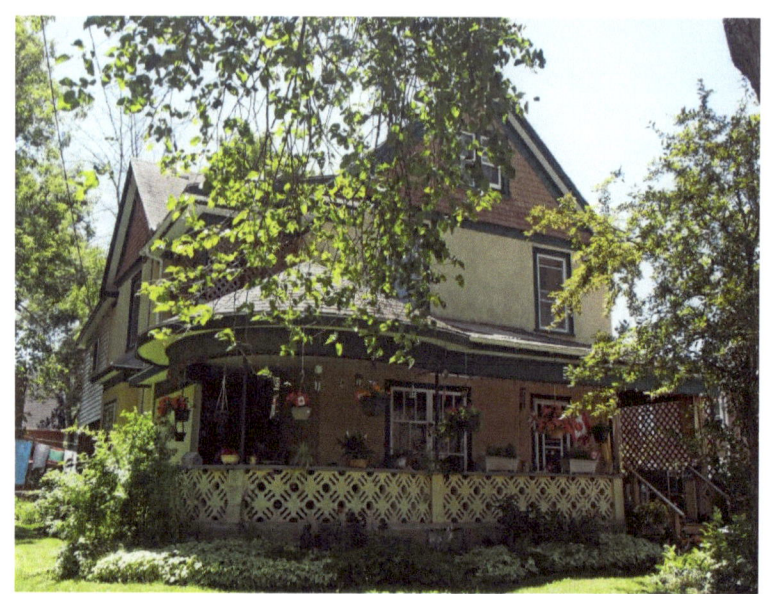

Maple Avenue

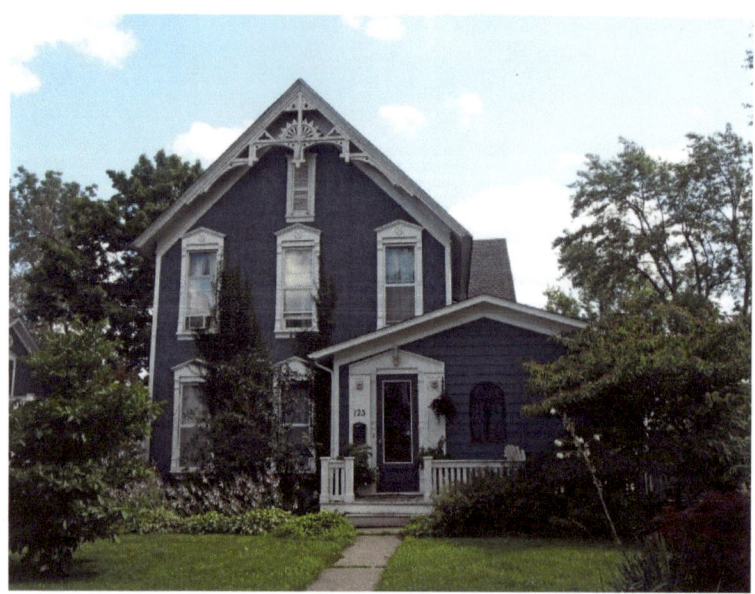

123 Merritt Street West – Gothic, verge board trim on gable

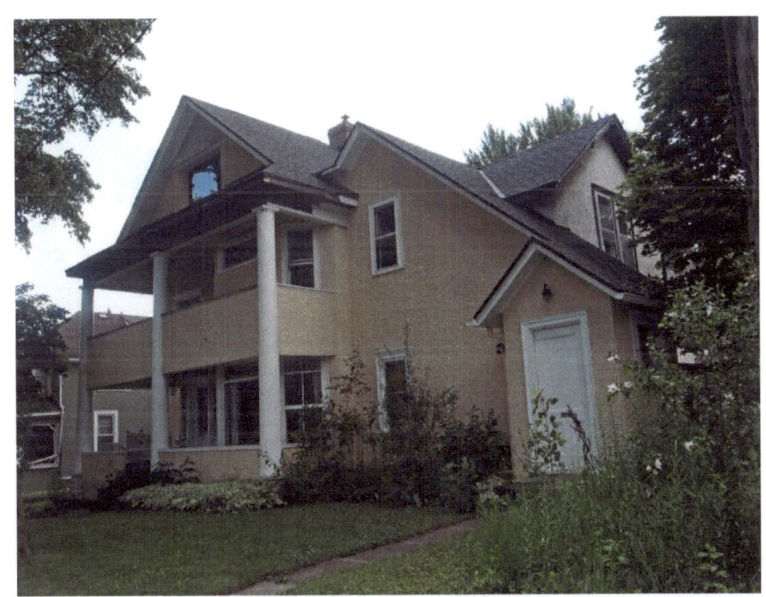

Merritt Street West

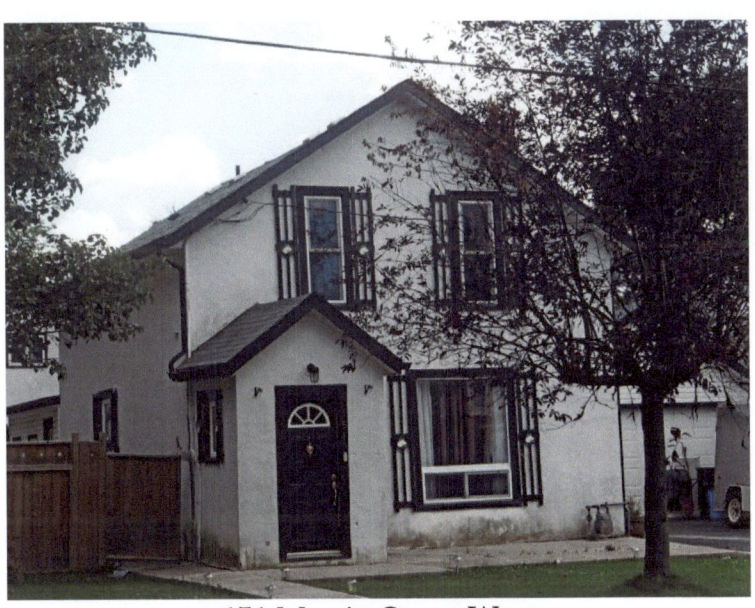

151 Merritt Street West

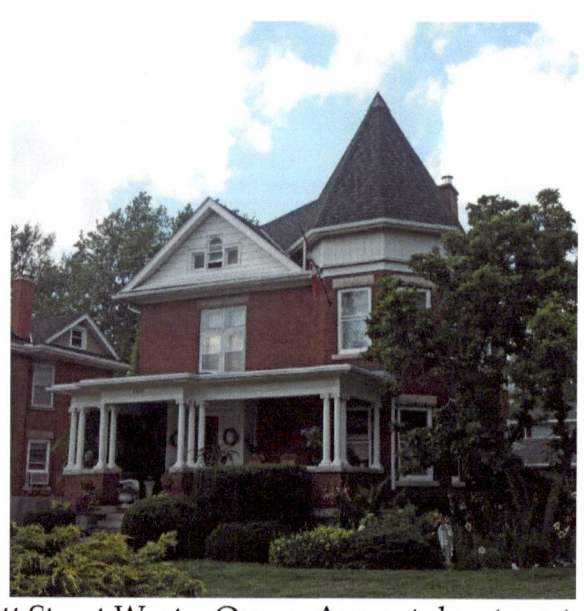

160 Merritt Street West – Queen Anne style – turret, Palladian
window in gable, Ionic capitals on pillared verandah

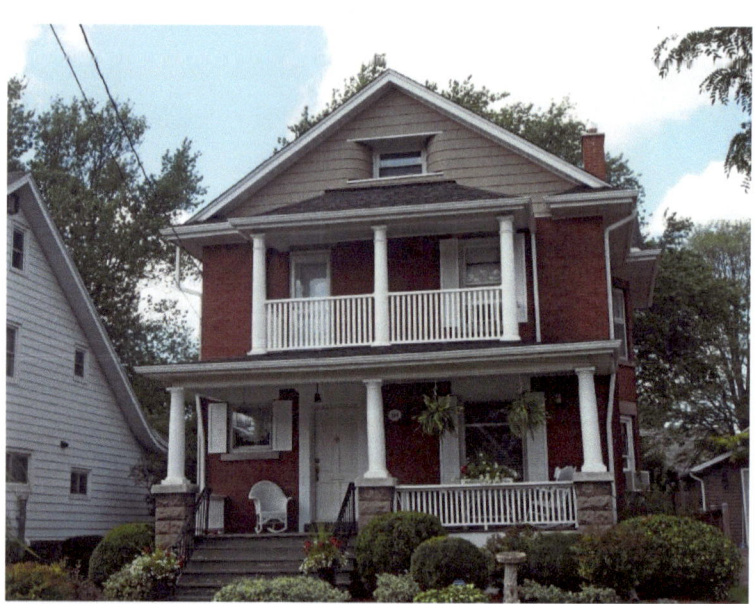

164 Merritt Street West – two-storied Doric pillared verandahs

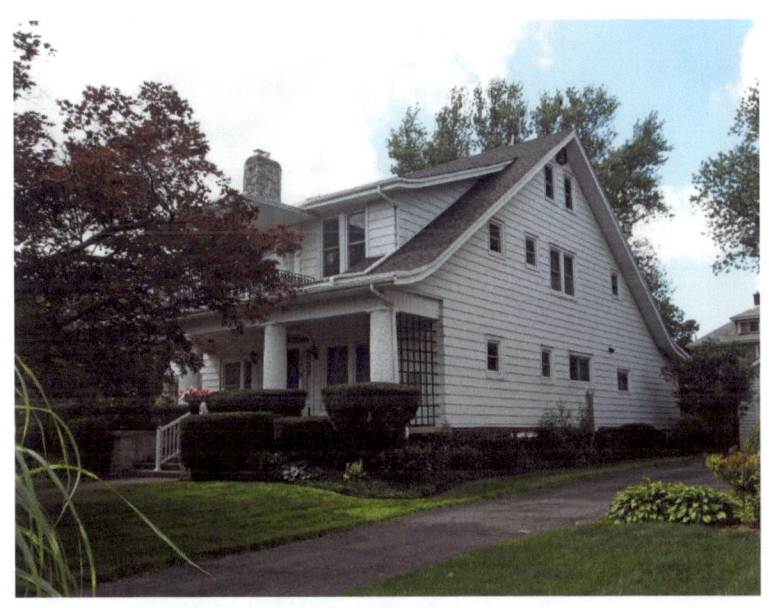

170 Merritt Street West – saltbox style, shed dormer, bay window

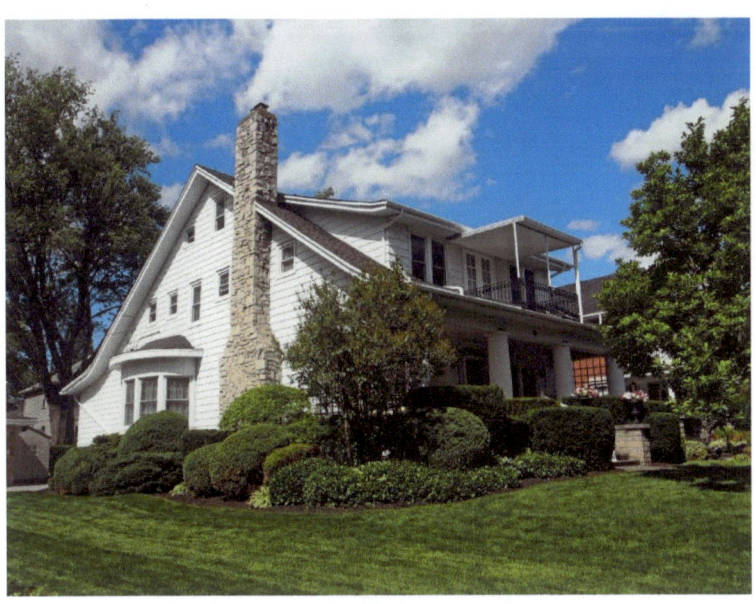

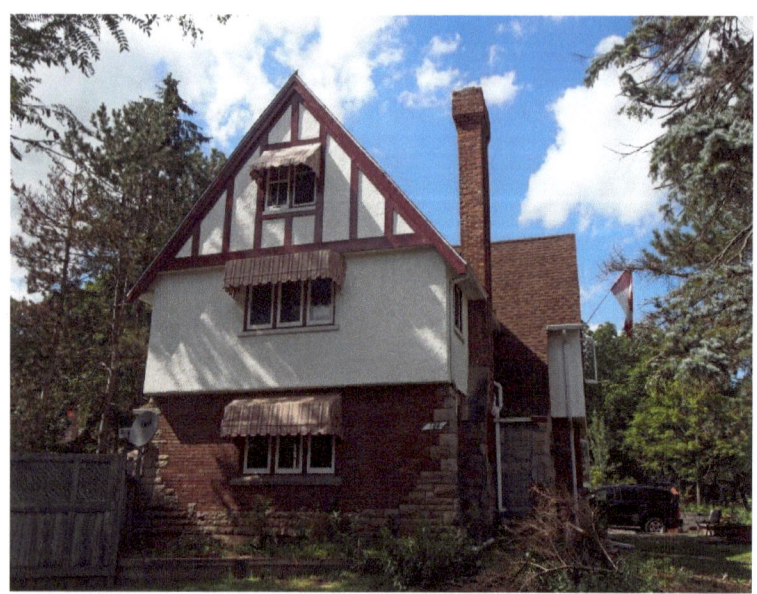

184 Merritt Street West – Tudor half-timbering style

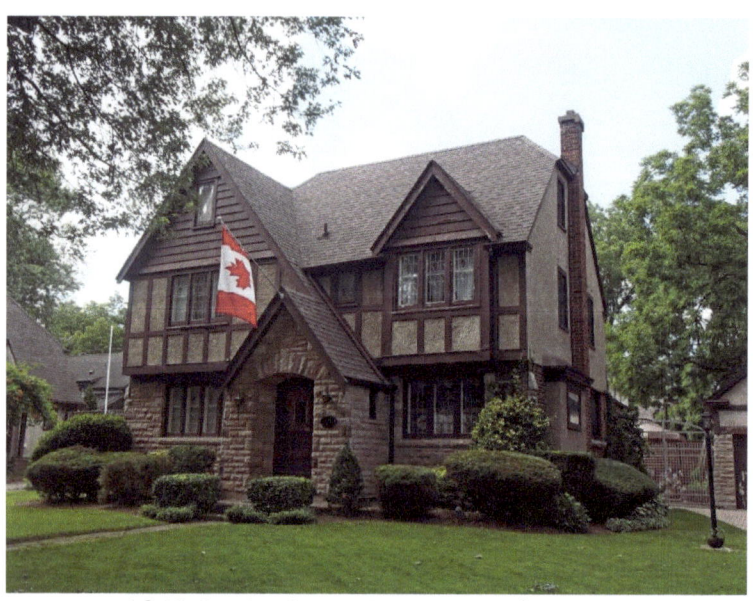

194 Merritt Street West – Tudor style

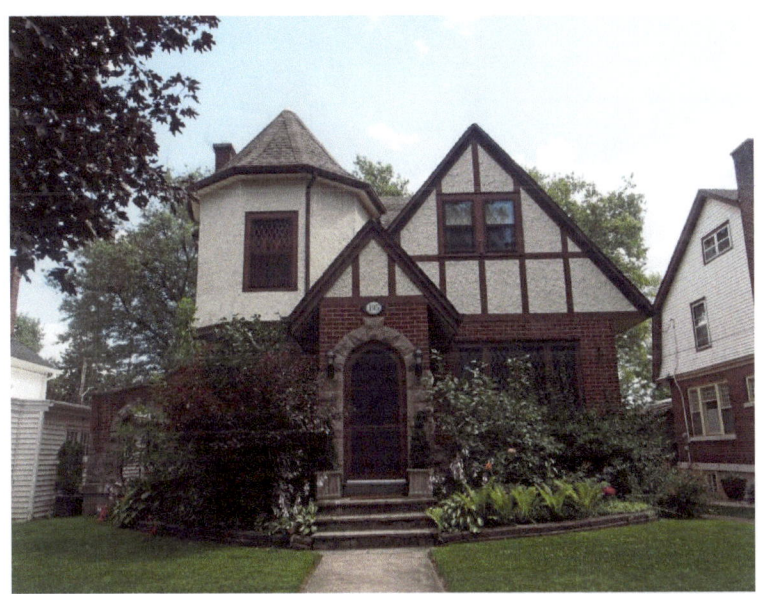

195 Merritt Street West – Tudor style, turret

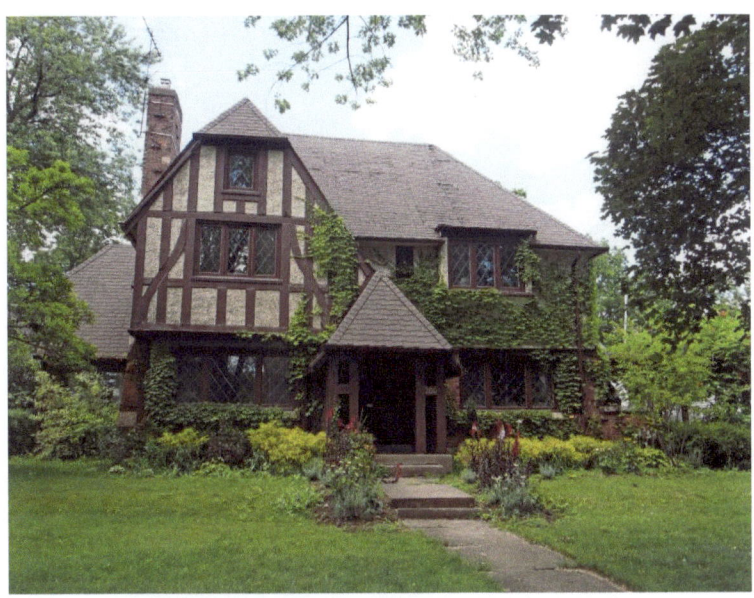

200 Merritt Street West – Tudor style

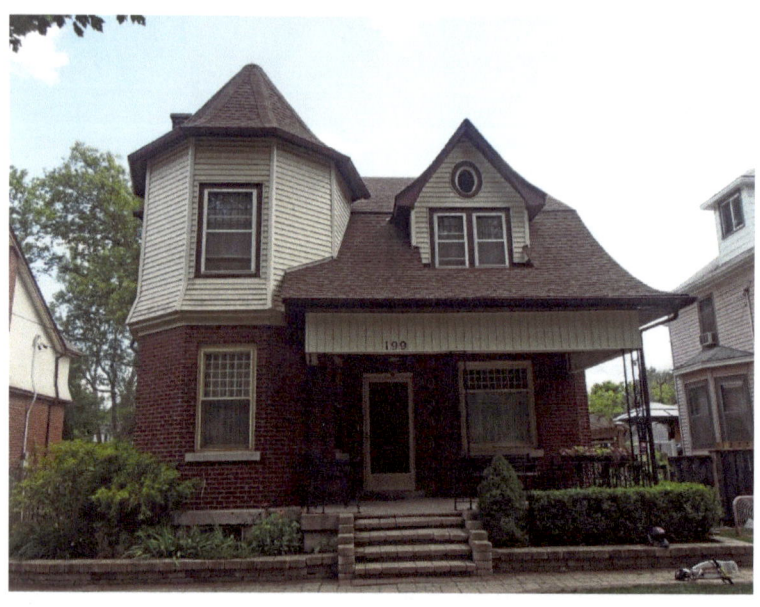

199 Merritt Street West – vernacular style, two-storey turret, dormer

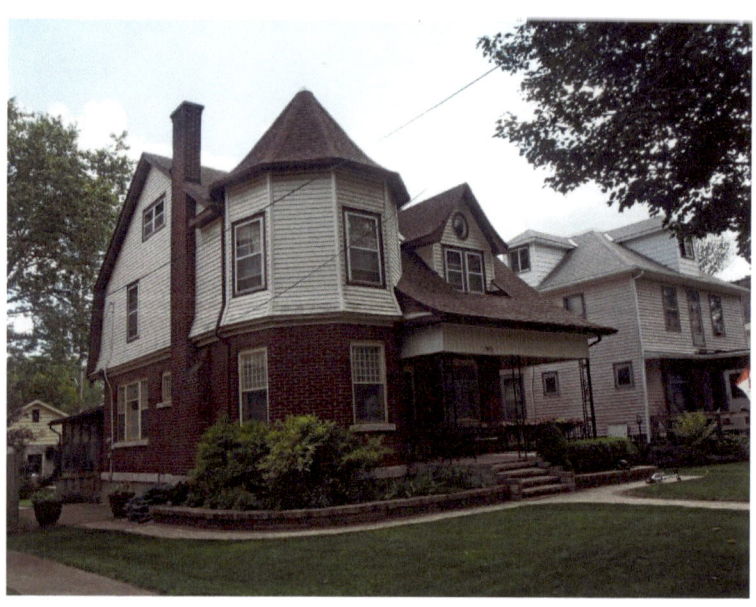

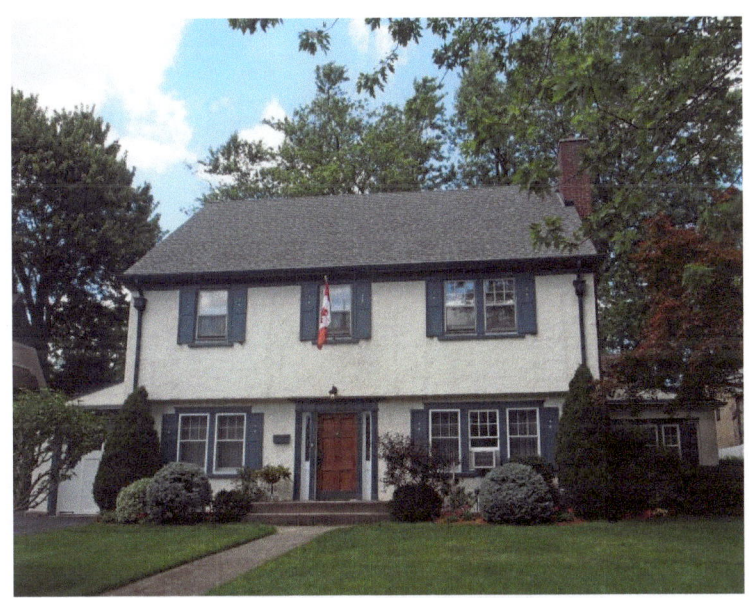

212 Merritt Street West

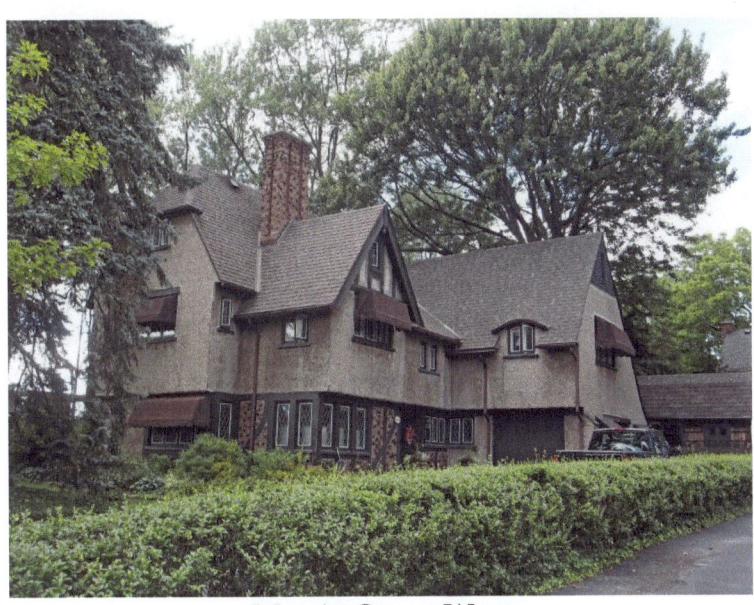

Merritt Street West

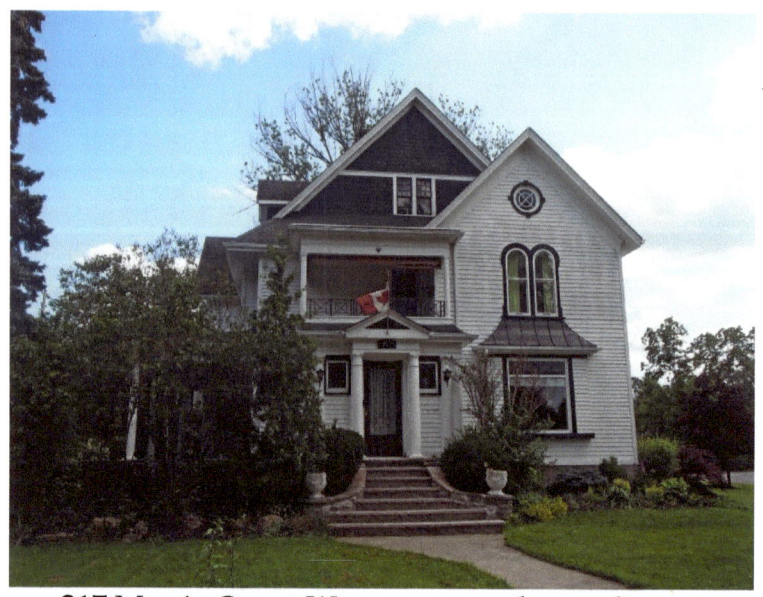

217 Merritt Street West – vernacular, pediment

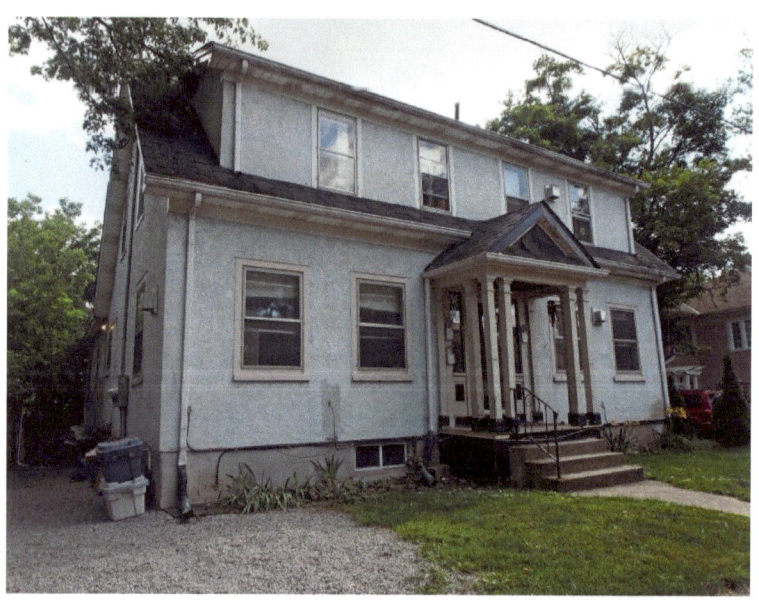

44 Merritt Street West – shed dormer, pediment above pillared porch

Mr. Thaddeus Hooker of New York set up the Hooker Brick Company at the base of Frazer Street where one million bricks and 100,000 drain tiles were produced annually. Hooker bricks were known for their quality and many of Welland's oldest businesses and brick homes were built of them. The plant employed 12 to 15 full-time men and used large quantities of cordwood.

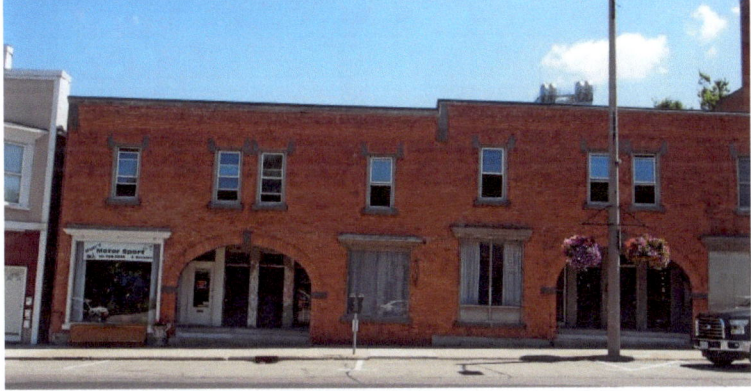

Niagara Street

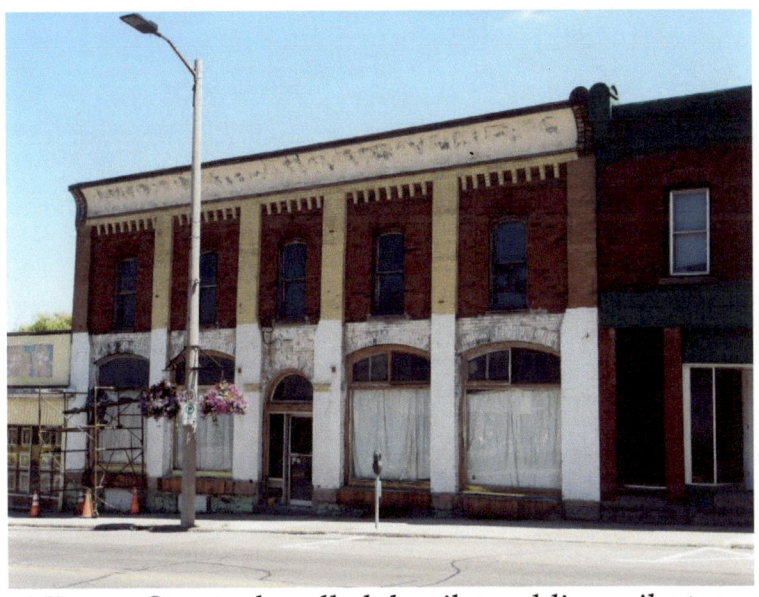

Niagara Street – bevelled dentil moulding, pilasters

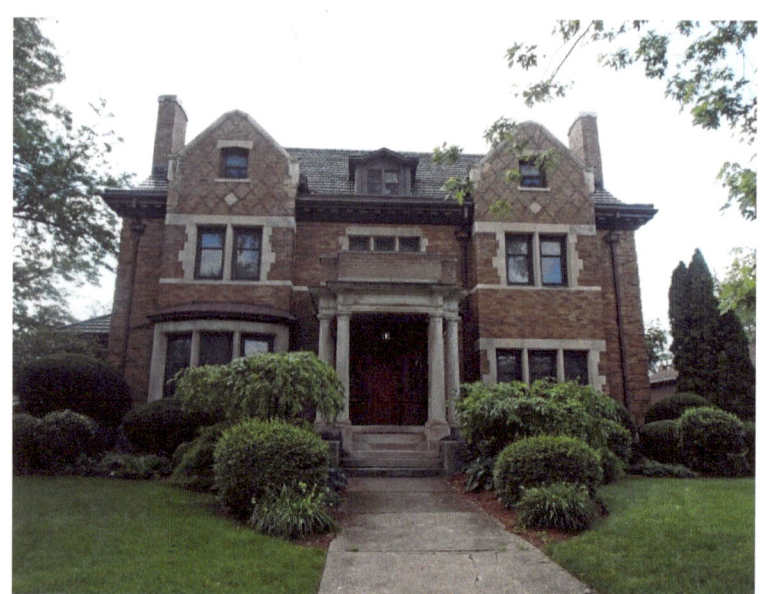

201 Niagara Street – Cooper Mansion – 1913-1914 - Renaissance Revival style, Jacobean gables (parapet), symmetrical façade with projecting wings, , dormers, stone trim, neoclassical doorway with elliptical fanlight and slender sidelights sheltered by a classical portico supported on six Doric columns

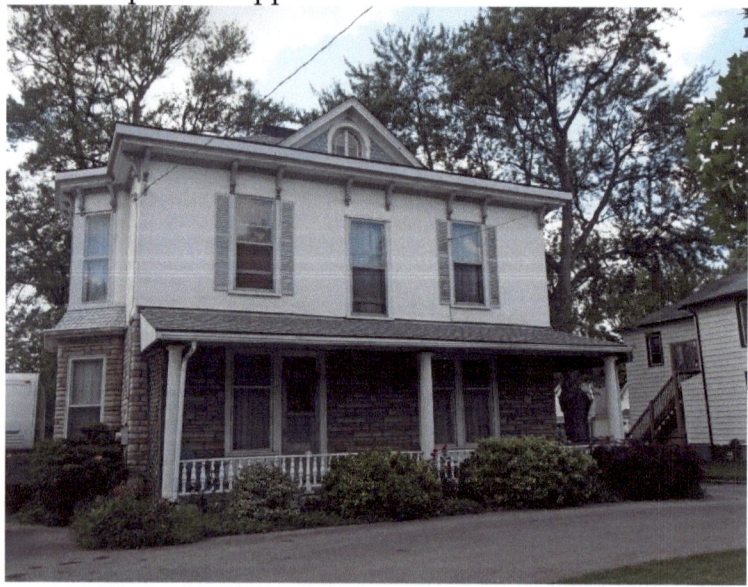

Niagara Street – Italianate, cornice brackets

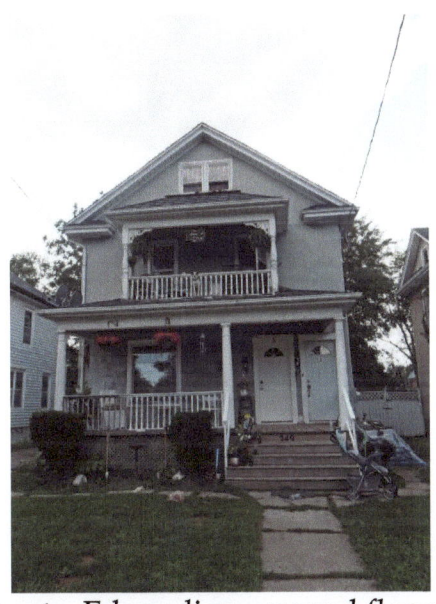

249 Niagara Street – Edwardian - second floor sleeping porch

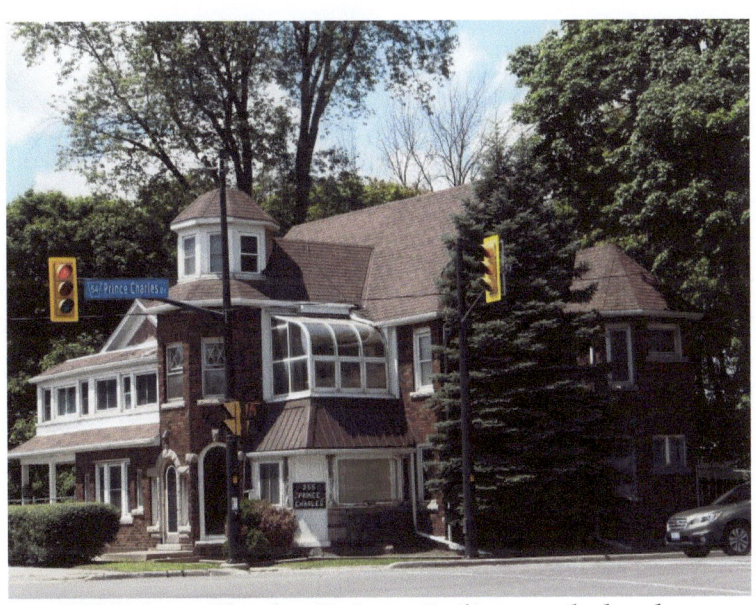

255 Prince Charles Drive – Italianate, belvedere

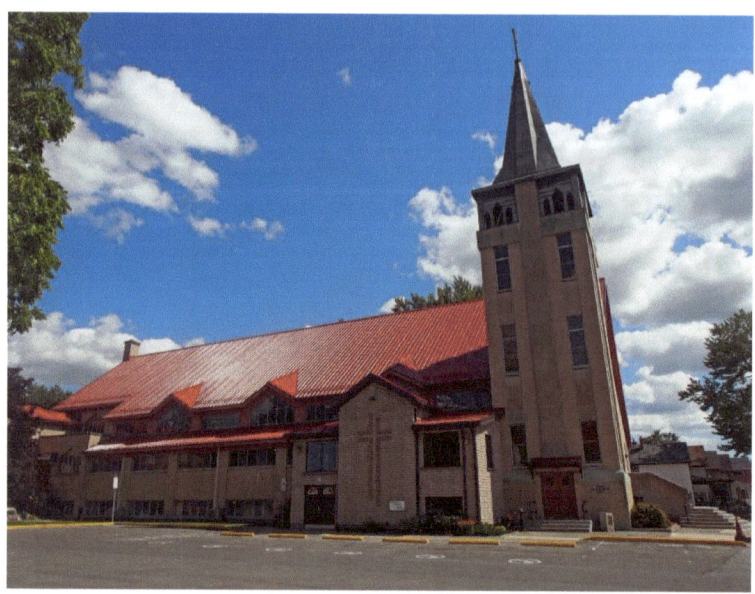

72 rue Empire - Paroisse Sacre-Coeur

## French Community in Welland

The neighbourhood that became commonly known as "French Town" was established in this area in 1918 when about twenty French-Canadian families arrived from Quebec to work at the Empire Cotton Mills plant. The Roman Catholic parish of Sacre-Coeur was established in 1920 and became the cultural centre of the francophone community that developed around Empire Street. More French-Canadian families arrived from Quebec, New Brunswick and northern Ontario throughout the 1920s. Another wave of Francophones moved here at the outset of the Second World War, attracted largely by employment opportunities in local industry. The French district was a strong and vibrant community that protected and fostered French-Canadian language and culture.

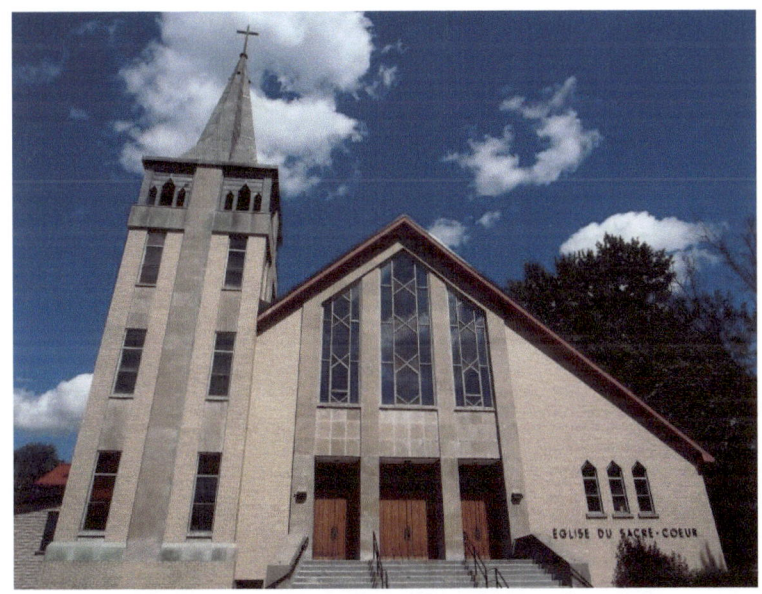

72 rue Empire - Paroisse Sacre-Coeur

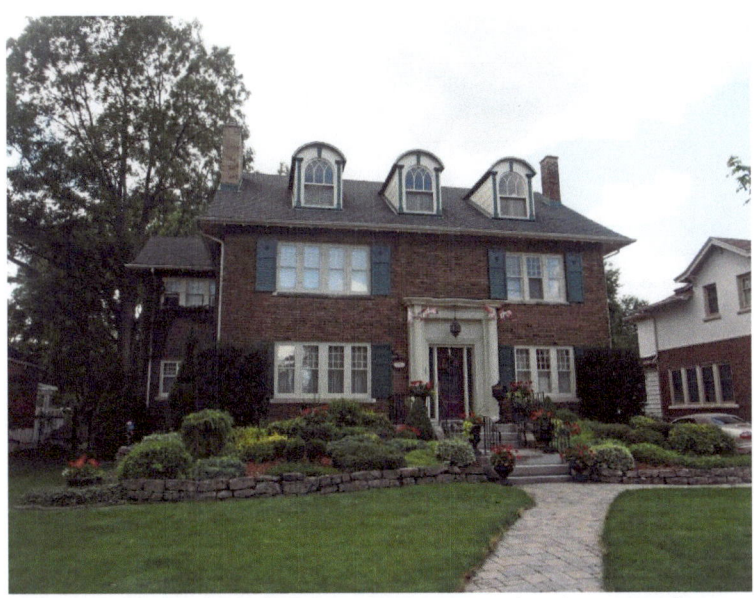

75 Shotwell Street – Italianate, engaged columns, dormers

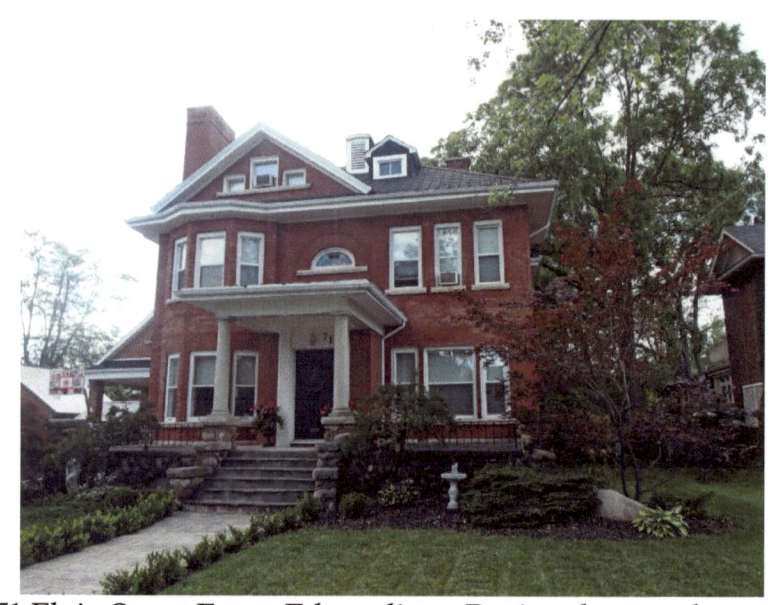

71 Elgin Street East – Edwardian - Doric columns, dormer, Palladian-type window in gable

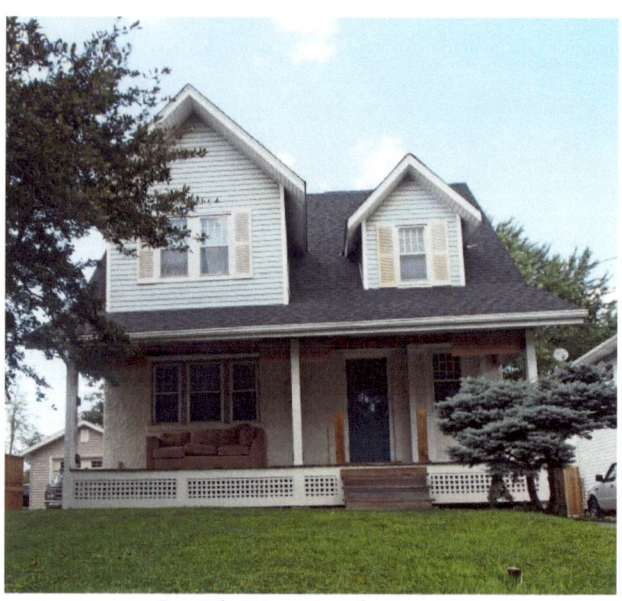

Smith Street - dormers

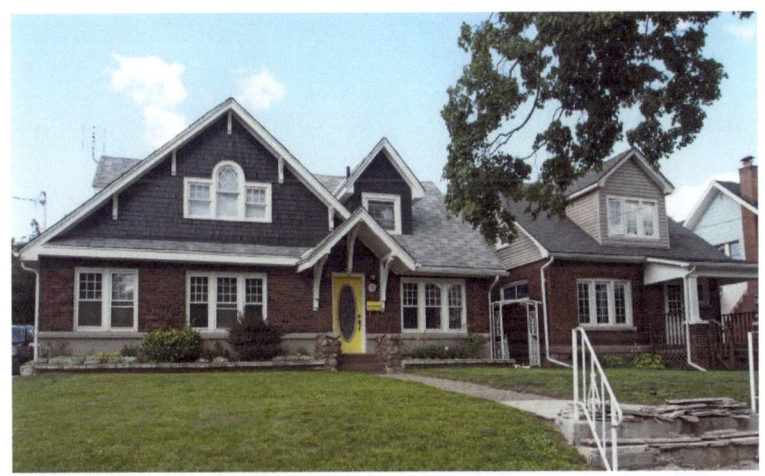

16 Smith Street – vernacular – Palladian window, brackets

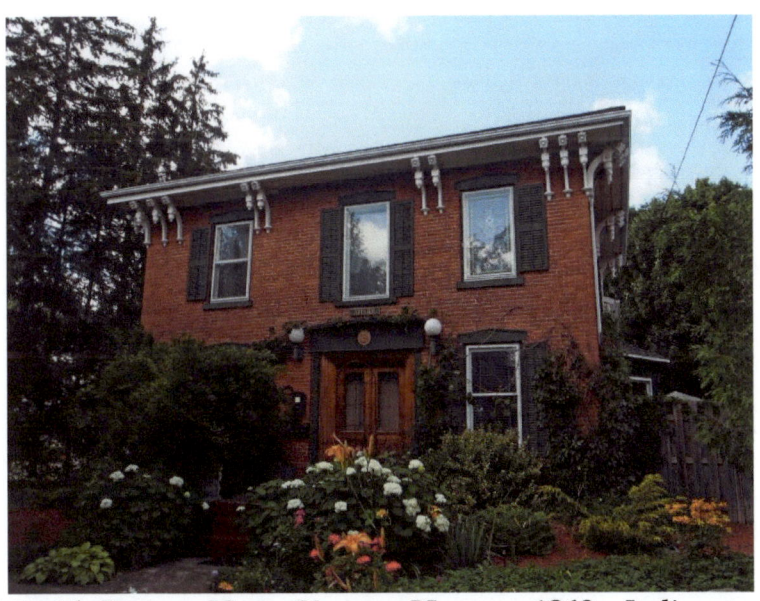

4 Smith Street – Haun-Kenney House – 1860 – Italianate –
cube shape, hipped roof, deeply projecting eaves, pendant
eave brackets grouped in twos and threes

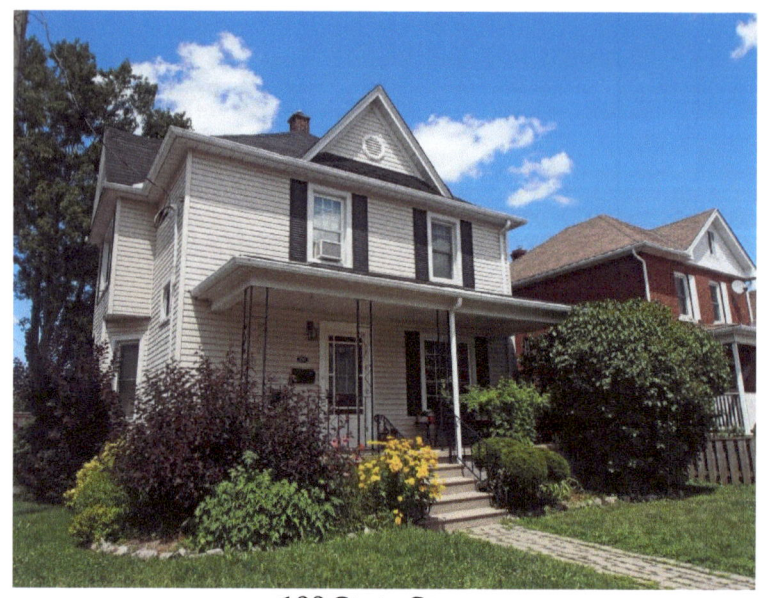

100 State Street

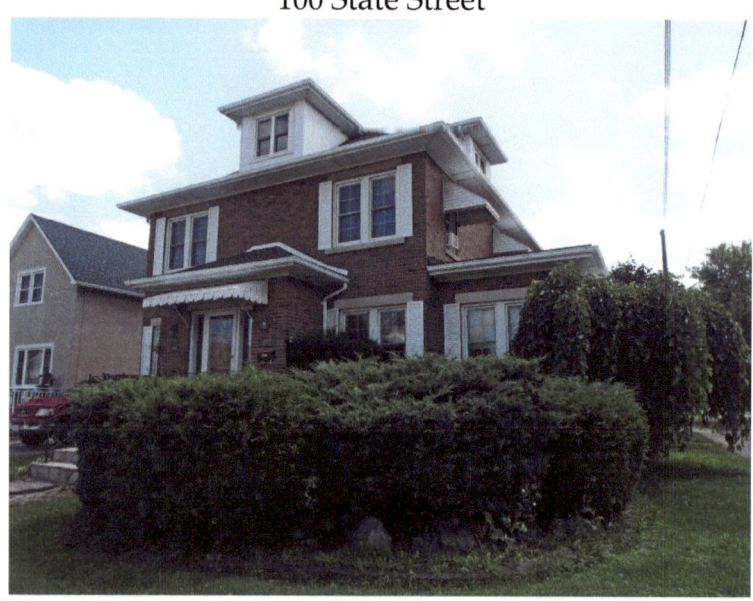

103 State Street – LoBosco-Foote house built in 1931 – shows strong influences of the Prairie style of architecture with its strong horizontal eave line, windows grouped in twos and threes, tall chimney

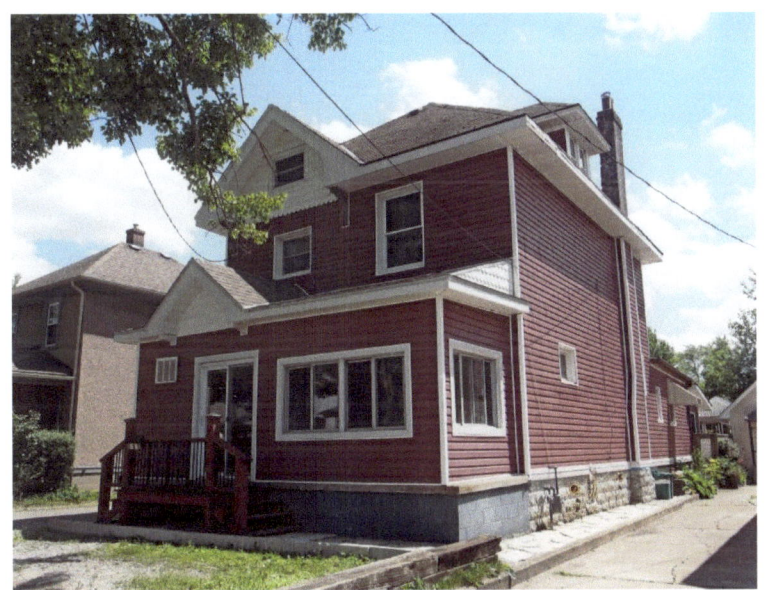

State Street

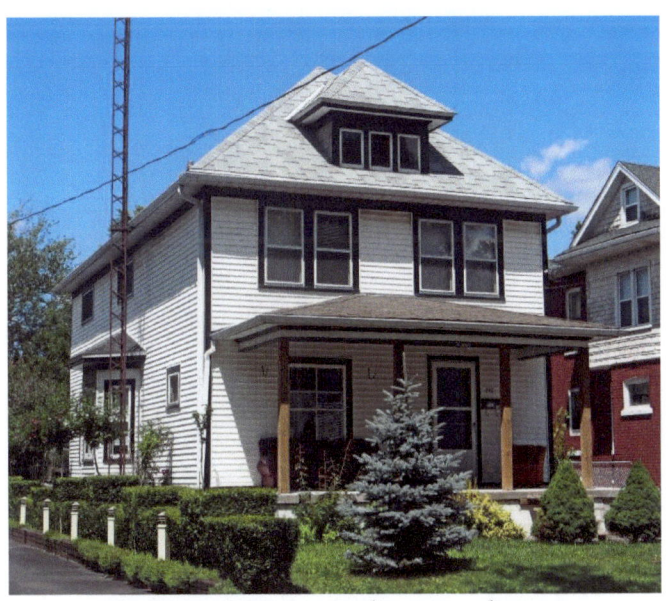

146 State Street – Italianate, dormer

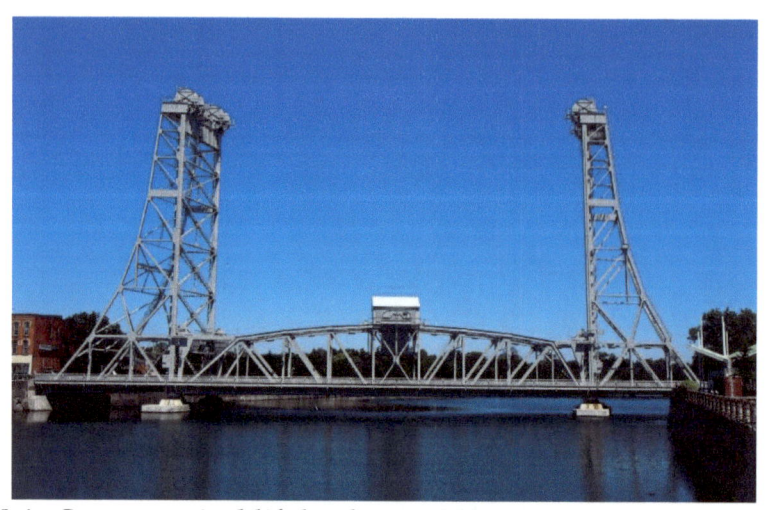

Main Street vertical lift bridge – 1927 - twin towers rise to a height of 170 feet providing a clearance of 120 feet

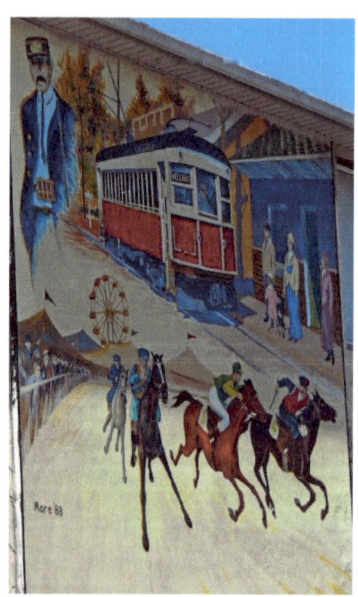

Mural

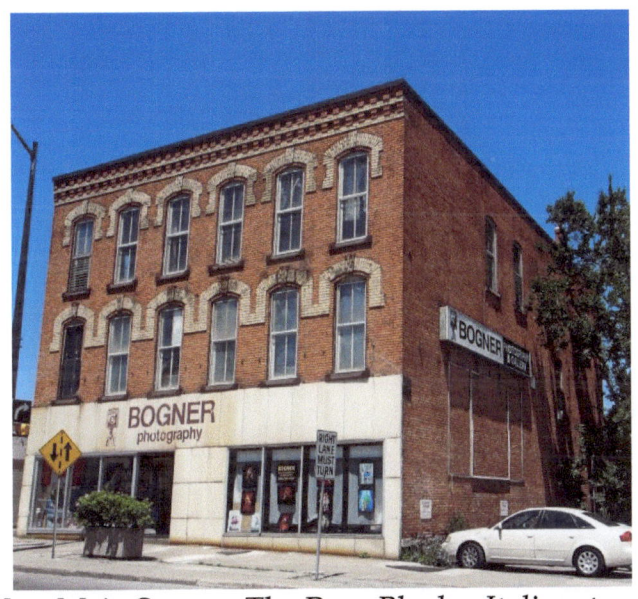

28 West Main Street – The Rose Block – Italianate – 1876
– 3-storey building constructed of brick from the
local Hooker brick company; accented semi-circular arches
above the windows with keystones

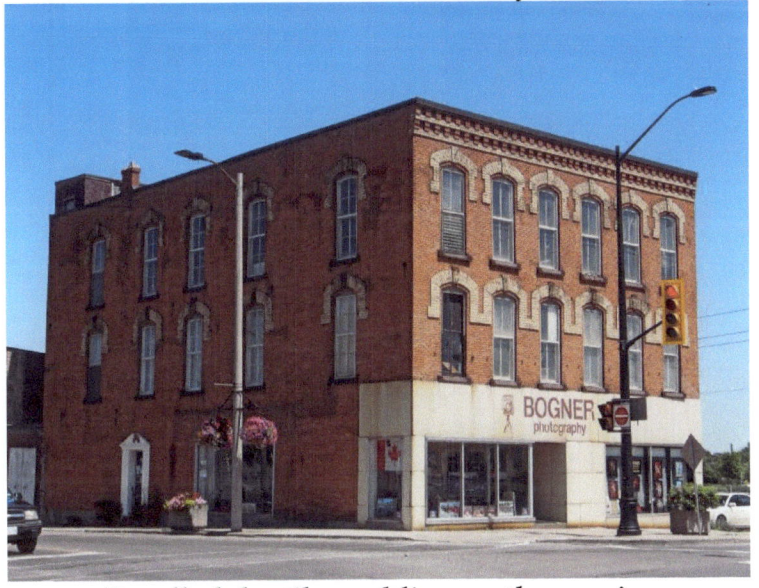

Bevelled dentil moulding on the cornice

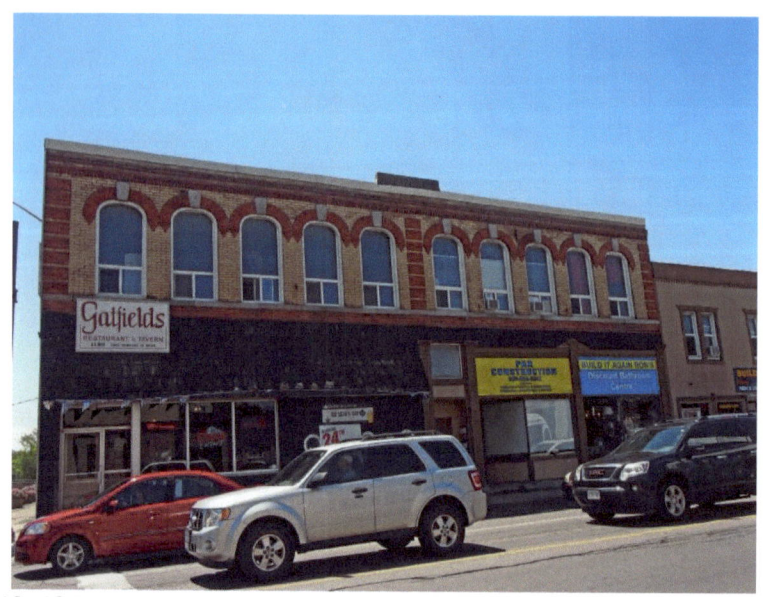

43-49 West Main Street – The Hobson Block – two-storey commercial block built of Hooker brick in 1877 – arched second-storey windows with keystones

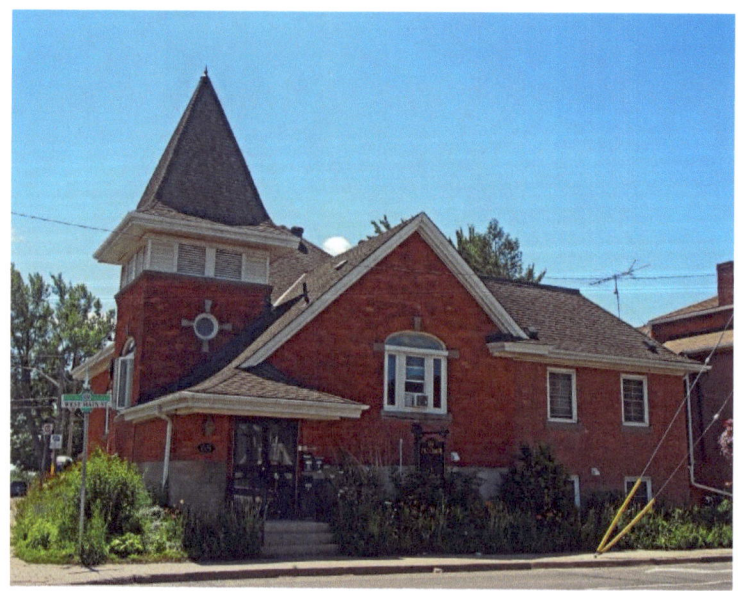

65 West Main Street – The Old Church - tower

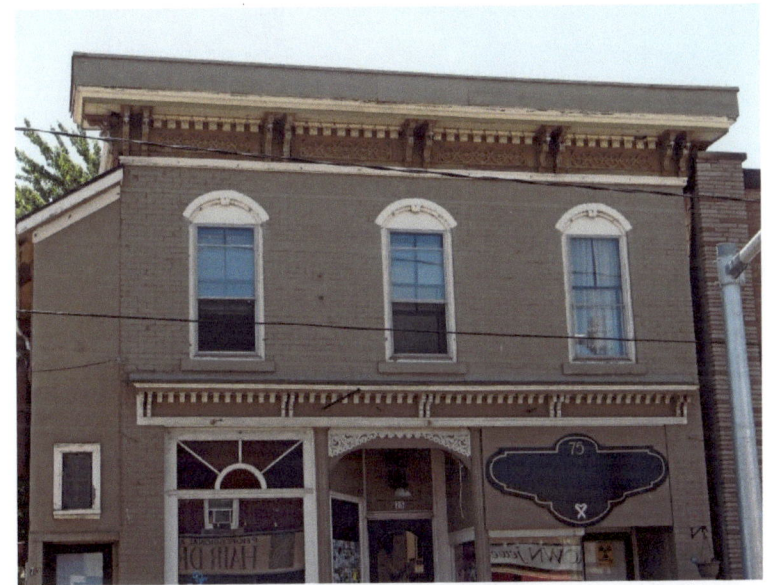

73-77 West Main Street – The Tuckey-Lee Building – Italianate - two-storey Hooker brick c. 1856 – semi-circular windows, paired cornice brackets under a pronounced cornice with dentil moulding

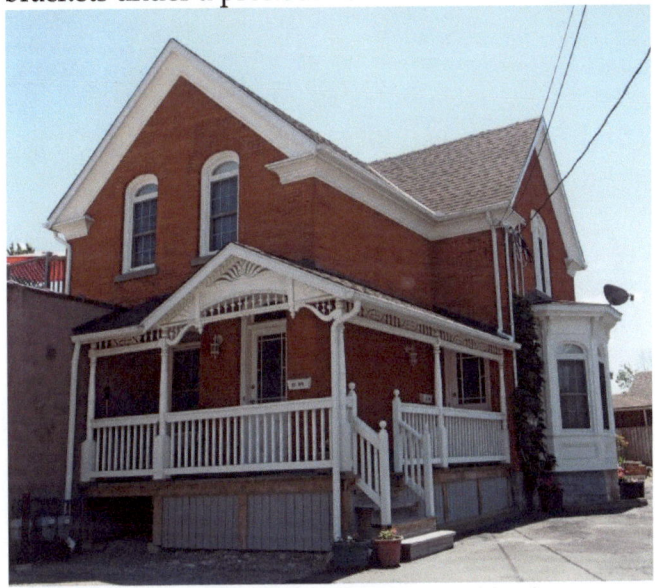

97 West Main Street – Italianate – two-storey Hooker orange brick – wooden frieze, elliptically-arched windows, ornate wood detailing, cornice return on gables

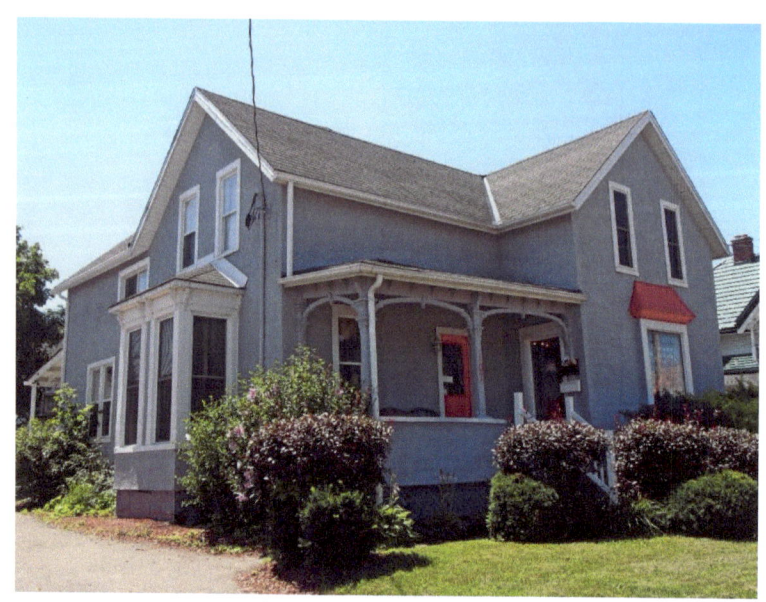

107 West Main Street

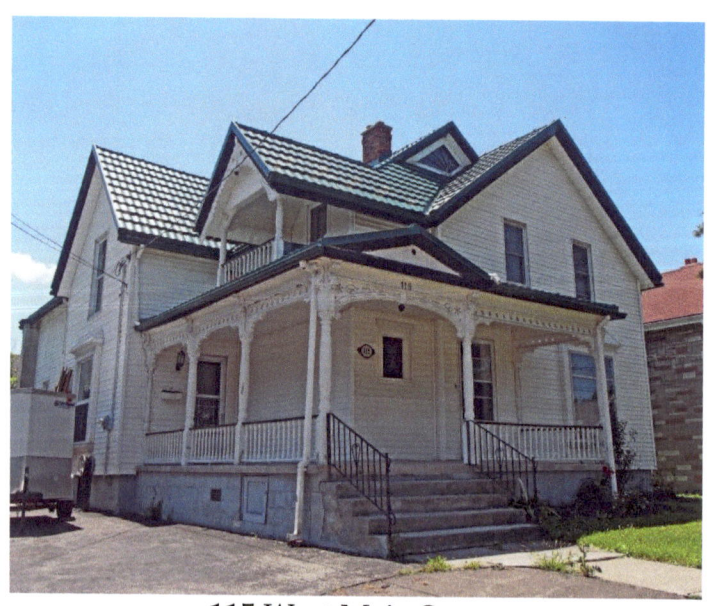

115 West Main Street

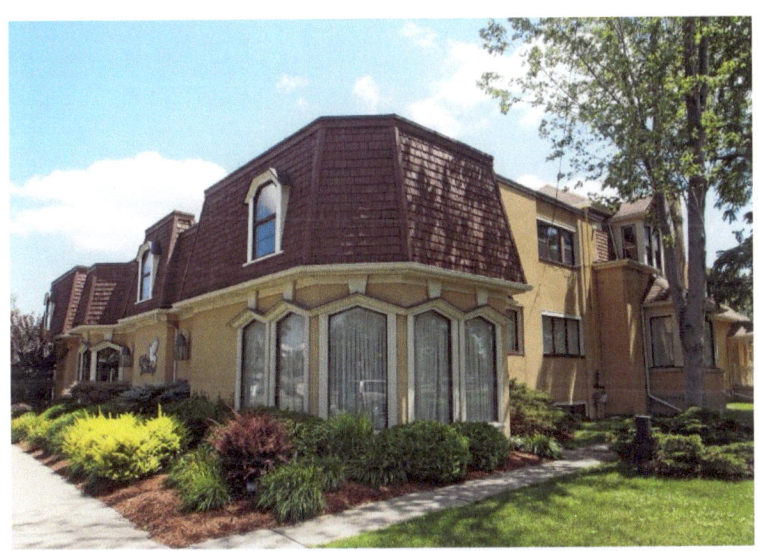

West Main Street – Cutney Funeral Chapel

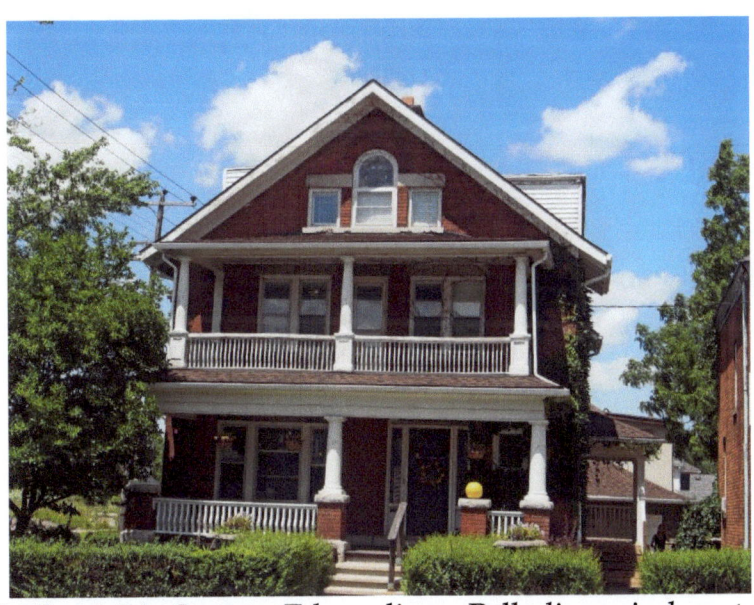

172 West Main Street – Edwardian – Palladian window, two-storey Doric columned verandahs

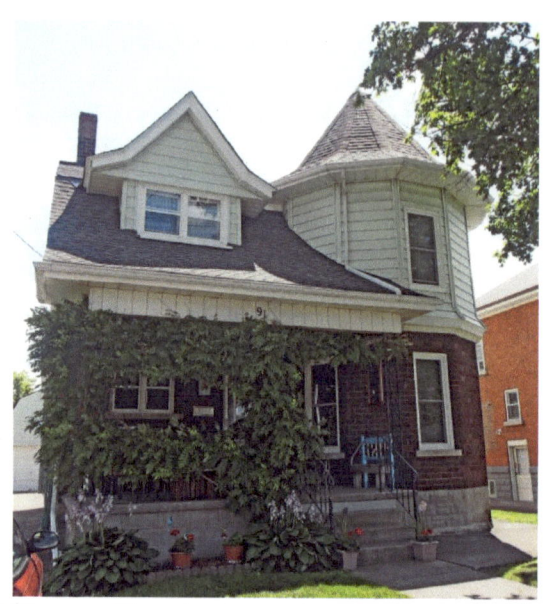

91 Young Street – two-storey turret, dormer

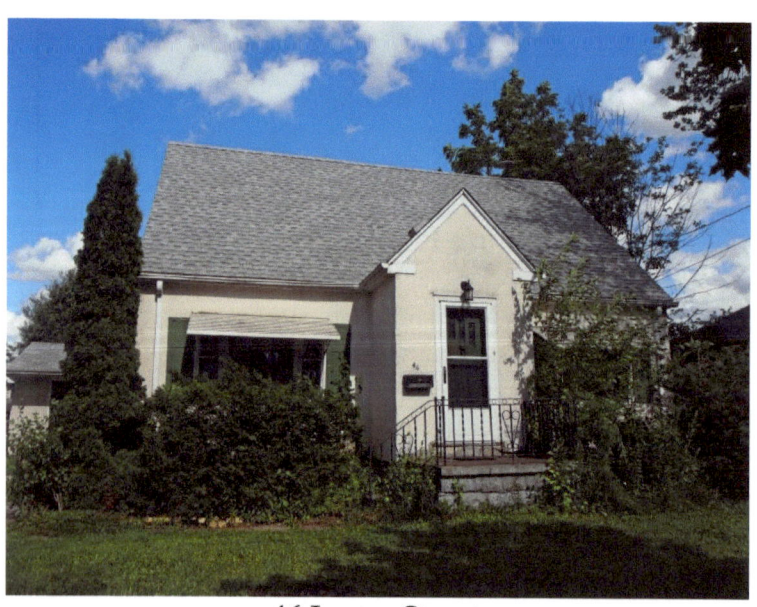

46 Lyons Street

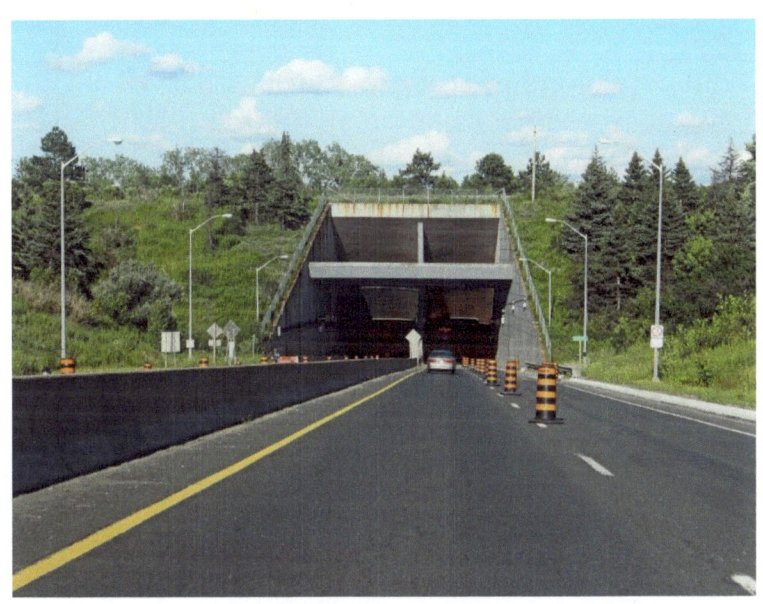

Tunnel under Welland Canal

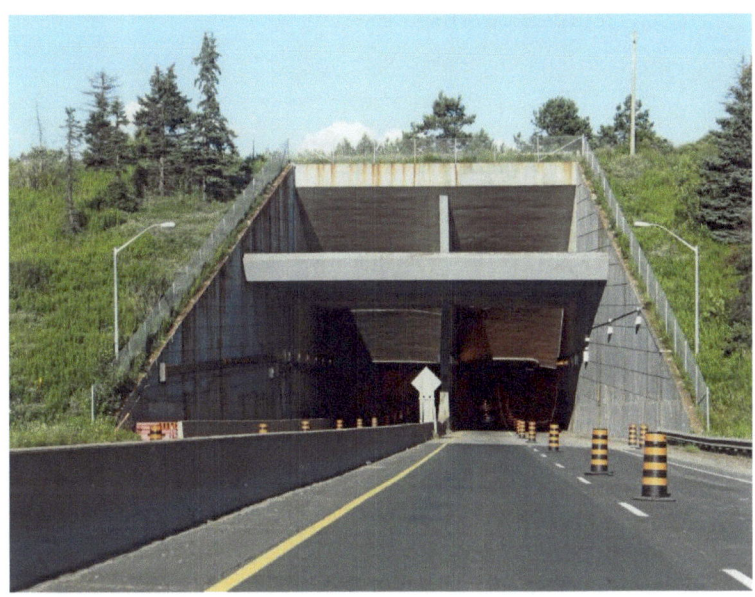

| | |
|---|---|
| **Bay Window:** A window that projects out from a wall, in a semicircular, rectangular, or polygonal design. Used frequently in Gothic and Victorian designs.<br><br>Example: 170 Merritt Street West, Page 25 | 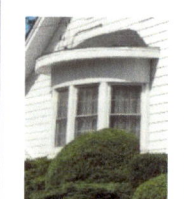 |
| **Belvedere**: (from the Italian "beautiful view") an architectural feature on a roof, in a garden or on a terrace that gives a beautiful view.<br><br>Example: 255 Prince Charles Drive, Page 33 | 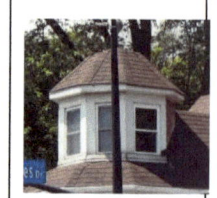 |
| **Brackets**: a decorative or weight-bearing structural element which forms a right angle with one side against a wall and the other under a projecting surface such as an eave or roof.<br><br>Example: 4 Smith Street, Page 37 | 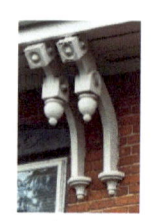 |
| **Buttress**: a masonry structure built against or projecting from a wall which serves to support or reinforce the wall. In Canadian architecture, they are sometimes used for decoration.<br><br>Example: King Street, Page 12 | 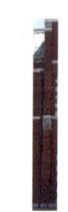 |

| | |
|---|---|
| **Capital:** The uppermost finish or decoration on a column. An Ionic column has a small base, a thin elegant shaft, and a capital composed of volutes which are carved whirls or twists that take the form of a scroll.<br>Example: 160 Merritt Street West, Page 24<br><br>A Doric column is characterized by a plain column with no base, a shaft with twenty flutings, and a simple capital with a simple entablature.<br>Example: 164 Merritt Street West, Page 24 | 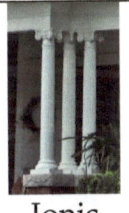<br>Ionic<br><br>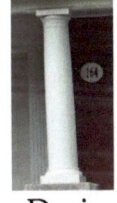<br>Doric |
| **Columns** were initially created to support a roof and porch structure. Originally they were free standing. Over time, builders began to build the walls between the columns so that the columns were part of the wall itself. These are called engaged columns. Engaged columns can be either structural or decorative.<br>Example: 75 Shotwell Street, Page 35 | 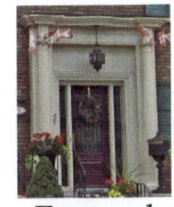<br>Engaged columns |
| **Cornice**: originally the wooden overhang of the roof. With the use of stone, brick, iron and steel, the cornice is any projecting shelf at the top of a ceiling or roof. They can be very decorative.<br>Example: 73-77 West Main Street, Page 43 | 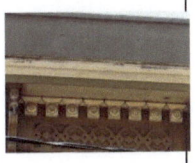 |
| **Cornice Return:** decorative element on the end of a gable.<br><br>Example: 97 West Main Street, Page 43 | 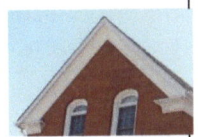 |
| **Dentil Moulding**: an even series of rectangles used as ornamental decoration in cornices.<br>Example: 28 West Main Street, Page 41 | 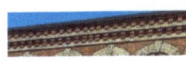 |

| | |
|---|---|
| **Dichromatic brickwork**: the use of two colours of brick, tile or slate to decorate a façade.<br><br>Example: 28 West Main Street, Page 41 | 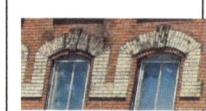 |
| **Dormer**: (French for "sleep") a gable end window that pierces through the plane of a sloping roof surface to create usable space in the top floor or attic of a building by adding headroom.<br>Example: 199 Merritt Street West, Page 28 | 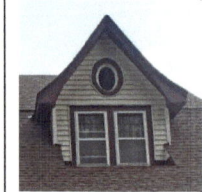 |
| **Gable**: the triangular portion of a wall between the edges of a sloping roof.<br>**Jacobean Gable:** the gable extends above the roofline.<br>Example: 72 Maple Avenue, Page 19 | 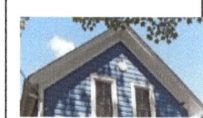 |
| **Keystones and Voussoirs**: a voussoir is a wedge-shaped element used in building an arch. A keystone is the central stone that locks all the stones into position, allowing the arch to bear weight. A keystone is often enlarged and embellished.<br>Example: 43-49 West Main Street, Page 42 | 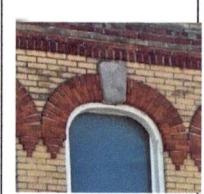 |
| **Palladian Window**: a large window that is divided into three sections with the centre section larger than the two side sections and usually arched.<br>Example: 16 Smith Street, Page 37 | 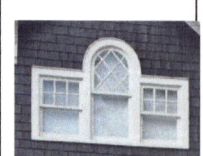 |
| **Pediment**: a triangular section above the horizontal structure (entablature), typically supported by columns. The inside of the triangle is called the tympanum.<br>Example: 44 Merritt Street West, Page 30 | 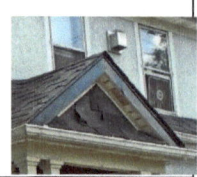 |

| | |
|---|---|
| **Pilaster**: a slightly projecting column built into or applied to the face of a wall for additional structural support.<br>Example: Niagara Street, Page 31 | |
| **Quoin**: masonry blocks at the corner of a wall, often a decorative feature, usually larger or of a different colour than the rest of the wall.<br><br>Example: King Street, Page 11 | |
| **Sidelight**: a window, usually with a vertical emphasis, that flanks a door, and is often used to emphasize the importance of a primary entrance.<br>Example: 201 Niagara Street, Page 32 | |
| **Turret:** a small tower that projects from the wall of a building.<br><br>Example: 91 Young Street, Page 46 | |
| **Verge board and Finial**: also called bargeboards – hang from the projecting end of a roof and are often elaborately carved and ornamented. **Finial:** ornament added to the top of a gable, pinnacle, canopy or spire – a Gothic element.<br>Example: 123 Merritt Street West, Page 22 | |

Building Styles

| | |
|---|---|
| **Beaux Arts**: Promoters of this style sought to express the classical principles on a grand and imposing scale.  Many of the Beaux Arts buildings were banks, post offices, and railway stations.  The Ontario Beaux Arts style is eclectic mixing elements of Classical, Renaissance and Baroque.  Often the designs have a temple-like façade, porticos with pediments, balustrades, and capitals in many styles.<br><br>Example: 140 King Street, Page 14 | 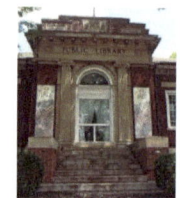 |
| **Edwardian**, 1900-1930 – This style bridges the ornate and elaborate styles of the Victorian era and the simplified styles of the 20th century.  Balanced facades, simple roof lines, dormer windows, large front porches, and smooth brick surfaces are its characteristics.<br><br>Example: 172 West Main Street, Page 45 | 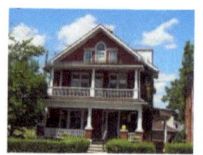 |
| **Gothic Revival**, 1830-1890 – These decorative buildings have sharply-pitched gables with highly detailed verge boards, pointed-arch window openings, and dichromatic brickwork. It is a common style in Ontario.<br><br>Example: 123 Merritt Street West, Page 22 | 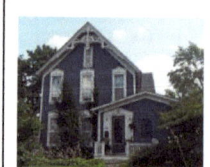 |

| | |
|---|---|
| **Italianate**, 1850-1900 – A two story rectangular building with a mild hip roof, a projecting frontispiece, and generous eaves with ornate cornice brackets was the basis of the style; often there are large sash windows, quoins, ornate detailing on the windows, belvederes and wraparound verandahs. Italianate commercial buildings often have cast iron cresting and elegant window surrounds.<br><br>Example: 4 Smith Street, Page 37 | 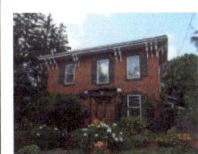 |
| **Queen Anne**, 1885-1900 – This style is distinguished by an irregular outline featuring a combination of an offset tower, broad gables, projecting two-storey bays, verandahs, multi-sloped roofs, and tall, decorative chimneys. A mixture of brick and wood is common. Windows often have one large single-paned bottom sash and small panes in the upper sash.<br><br>Example: 160 Merritt Street West, Page 24 | 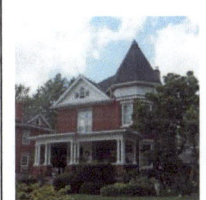 |

| | |
|---|---|
| **Renaissance Revival** (1870 - 1910) - The Renaissance Palazzo was a three or four storey building with a rusticated (very large masonry blocks with deep joints and decorated with rough or bold finishes) ground floor, and regularized understated windows on two upper levels, always finished by an elaborate cornice. The Renaissance saw the development of a graceful and balanced adaptation of the Greek styles.  In Ontario, the Renaissance was revived in commercial buildings, banks, offices, and churches in many towns. Most of the Renaissance Revival buildings are designed without columns while those with columns and pilasters are more ornate.<br><br>Example: 201 Niagara Street, Page 32 | 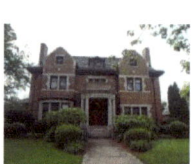 |
| **Romanesque Revival**, 1880-1910 – This style hearkens back to medieval architecture of the 11th and 12th centuries with a heavy appearance, blocky towers and rounded arches.<br>Example: 88 King Street, Page 13 | 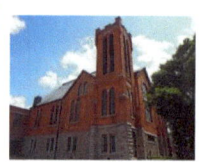 |

| | |
|---|---|
| **Saltbox**: A saltbox is a building with a long, pitched roof that slopes down to the back, generally a wooden frame house. A saltbox has just one storey in the back and two stories in the front. The asymmetry of the unequal sides and the long, low rear roof line are the most distinctive features of a saltbox, which takes its name from its resemblance to a wooden lidded box in which salt was once kept. The earliest saltbox houses were created when a lean-to addition was added onto the rear of the original house extending the roof line sometimes to less than six feet from ground level.<br>Example: 170 Merritt Street West, Page 25 | 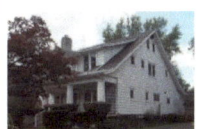 |
| **Tudor Revival** – exposed timbers with stucco infill, multi-paned windows.<br><br>Example: 194 Merritt Street West, Page 26 | 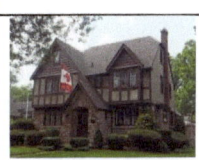 |
| **Vernacular/Traditional Mode** 1638 - 1950<br>Influenced but not defined by a particular style, vernacular buildings are made from easily available materials and exhibit local design characteristics.<br>Example: 217 Merritt Street West, Page 30 | 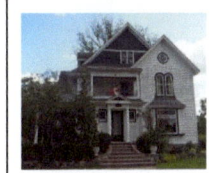 |
| **Victorian** - In Ontario, a Victorian style building can be seen as any building built between 1840 and 1900 that doesn't fit into any of the other categories. It encompasses a large group of buildings constructed in brick, stone, and timber, using an eclectic mixture of Classical and Gothic motifs.<br>Example: 60 Maple Avenue, Page 18 | 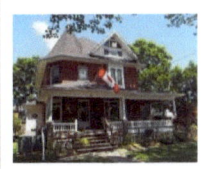 |